The Name's the Same is more than just a glossary of placenames – it is a simple yet poignant history of a migrating people.

Scottish journalist Stuart Conroy has painstakingly researched the detail of the Scottish diaspora and has followed up every Bothwell and Banff, every Edinburgh and Dunedin, every Aberdeen and Ayr.

The result is the most exhaustive listing of overseas Scottish placenames yet compiled.

Stuart Conroy has researched the whys and wherefores behind the imprint of Scottish placenames on the globe. In a series of engrossing chapters, he reveals how these names were adopted in far-flung places and he writes about the human stories behind the mass migration of Scots to all parts of the world.

the Name's the Same

Scottish Placenames Worldwide

Stuart Conroy

to my niece
Kaitlin Tottman

© Stuart Conroy

First published 1996
Argyll Publishing
Glendaruel
Argyll PA22 3AE
Scotland

**British Library Cataloguing-in-Publication
Data.
A catalogue record for this book is
available from the British Library.**

ISBN 1 874640 37 8

Origination
Cordfall Ltd, Glasgow

Printing
Bookcraft (Bath) Ltd

contents

introduction	9
Aberdeen	13
Ayrshire	20
The Scottish Borders	28
The Clyde	34
Dumfriesshire	41
Dundee	47
Edinburgh	53
Fife	63
Glasgow	68
Highlands	79
Western Isles	87
Orkney & Shetland	95
Inverness	97
Lanarkshire	101
Lothian	112
Perth	115
Renfrew	123
Stirlingshire	128
Gazetteer	135

acknowledgements

I would like to thank all those who have helped me in my research and preparation of this book, in particular my father, Harry Conroy, who inspired the writing of *The Name's the Same.*

His guidance, patience and support throughout two years of research has largely contributed to what is the most exhaustive list of Scottish placenames worldwide.

Thanks to Derek Rodger, my publisher, for his hard work in bringing the book from its early stages through to the final completion.

I would like to acknowledge the excellent assistance offered to me by the libraries, councils and residents from many of the towns and cities around the world that have their details included. Obviously to mention here all those who went out of their way to supply me with information would involve another list of book length.

Staff in the Mitchell Library in Glasgow, Scotland were especially helpful.

Stuart Conroy
Glasgow, Scotland
May 1996

a Scotsman on the frontier –
the first house in Glasgow, Montana (1887)
on the site of the present day City–County Library
Courtesy Montana Historical Society, USA

introduction

Over the centuries Scots have emigrated from every part of their homeland to countries all around the world. Although Scotland has a population of only 5 million people there are an estimated 90 million emigré Scots worldwide. Scottish settlers and explorers have made their mark on the world map by naming new lands after their homes in Scotland. Villages, cities and counties, even rivers and mountains, now bear the names of their Scottish counterparts.

The diaspora abroad were often elevated to prominent positions, such as Sir Thomas McIllwraith who emigrated from Ayr to Australia in 1854, went on to become the State Premier of Queensland, Australia, and had a town named after his birthplace. Gilbert John Elliot Murray Kynynmound became Governor General of Canada in 1898, naming the town of Minto in New Brunswick. He was the 4th Earl of Minto and named the Canadian town after his family seat in Scotland.

Much of the financing for the North American railroads was raised by Scots in Scotland. The Canadian Pacific Railroad was financed by Sir Hugh Allan, the owner of the Allan Steamship Line which operated from the Clyde. The Western Union Railroad was financed by bankers from Lanark, Scotland. John H MacTavish who was Land Commissioner for the Canadian Pacific Railway was responsible for naming the town of Banff in Alberta after the Scottish town near the birthplace of the railway's president, Sir George Stephen.

Scots took up other key positions in the early settlements. They became postmasters and stationmasters and many of the new towns were surveyed by Scots. Others laid out town plans on the land they had worked for or been given.

It was mainly these proud Scots who were responsible for the naming of the new sites after their native Scottish homes.

There are numerous reasons why Scots decided to leave their homeland. Some chose to seek their fortune and careers overseas while others were encouraged by the availability of free land offered by the Colonial governments abroad. There was however a large number of these emigrants who had no choice but to leave their homeland.

The Highland Clearances are said to have begun as early as the 1730s with the elimination of the tacksmen from the traditional clan system in the Highlands. These clearances became more apparent in the 1760s when lowland sheep farmers acquired land in the Highlands, and gained momentum in the early nineteenth century when rents rose dramatically.

There are many towns such as Lochaber in Nova Scotia, Canada; Grampian in Pennsylvania, USA and Argyll in New South Wales, Australia which are a permanent reminder of those Scots who migrated from the Highlands of Scotland.

The Great Migration is said to have begun around the time of the Highland Clearances although Scots had been sailing to the New World for some time before. So much is owed to the Scottish adventurers who throughout the centuries explored and charted the new continents. Two of the most famous of Scottish explorers were the Arctic pioneer John Ross who named the Clyde River in Canada, and his nephew James Clark Ross who located the North Magnetic Pole.

The first attempts at Scottish settlements abroad was as early as 1622 when a small group of colonists from Galloway headed to Nova Scotia. A second ship followed in 1623 and although some exploration was achieved, the attempts at settlement were unsuccessful. Further settlement was attempted in 1635 by the Earl of Stirling and in 1647 there were plans for a Scottish settlement in Virginia. After the Civil War, between 1648 and 1652 there were a number of Scots Loyalists who were transported to the plantations in Barbados and Virginia and in 1666 during the reign of Charles II, the same fate befell over 1,700 Covenanters.

By the beginning of the eighteenth century most of the Scots in Virginia were either slaves, indentured labourers or servants, or tobacco factors. There was money to be made in the servant trade with America and in fact Aberdeen had a considerable American trade in the late seventeenth and early eighteenth centuries when people would be kidnapped and transported to be sold as servants. There were exiles after the 1715 Jacobite rebellion and once again after the 1745 rebellion when the British government banished around 1,000 rebels after the Jacobite defeat at the battle of Culloden in 1746. They were to serve as servants, mainly in South Carolina, Maryland, Virginia and Antigua.

And of course after the loss of the American colonies the first settlers in Australia were in fact criminals who had previously been transported to America. Not all of these criminals were guilty of a serious offence. In fact a number were transported from their homeland for their political beliefs.

The British government began to encourage emigration in the first half of the nineteenth century. In 1815 following defeat in the American War of Independence the government encouraged emigration to Canada in order to counteract American infiltration there. During the war many of the Scots Highlanders who had settled in America were Loyalists, so found themselves unwelcome among the revolutionaries.

Highlanders from Glengarry, Scotland had settled in America in 1773. They ended up in Glengarry! ie Glengarry County, Ontario where they established a settlement. In the years following the war there was also a new competitor as Australia began allowing free settlers into the land. Massive propaganda by the colonial government in Canada around this time included financial assistance to attract settlers.

When news reached Britain that gold had been discovered in Victoria, Australia in the 1850s, towns quickly sprang up as thousands of emigrants flocked into the area to make their fortune. One particular town was named after Rutherglen, Scotland. It grew up around the Wahgunyah run and within six months of the first payable gold being found 15,000 people were on the goldfields.

Emigration was now known to be big business and some made a personal fortune out of the emigrants such as Sir Hugh Allan whose company, the Allan Steamship Line brought out many emigrants from the British Isles during the 1880s and 1890s. In 1888 the Allan Company picked up forty five families from the Outer Hebrides and mainland of Scotland. They sailed from Glasgow on the 26th March, 1889 on the Allan Liner *Mayflower*, and in 1893 the group of emigrants named the town of Saltcoats, Saskatchewan, in honour of his birthplace in Scotland.

Some agents were totally unscrupulous and made promises which they simply could not keep. Pamphlets circulating in Ayrshire in the 1770s promised that rents in Prince Edward Island would rise during seven years from 2 pennies to 2 shillings an acre and "never after to be raised". Another agent tricked a party from the Chisholm territory to go to Nova Scotia where they believed they would find a tree to yield sugar, soap and even fuel. He led them to believe that America was only a short voyage from the Western Isles. Some of the optimistic travellers inquired as they sighted the Outer Hebrides, "Is that America?"

Little did they know that they had a long journey ahead of them which took on average forty four days and it was not unknown for this travelling time to be doubled. Conditions on the emigrant ships were harsh, many of the passengers became sick and death was not an infrequent occurrence on the long journeys to the new world.

The part that Scotland played in developing the colonies of the British Empire in America, Canada, Australia, New Zealand and parts of Africa can be seen by simply picking up an Atlas. It is clear to see that Scottish placenames abound.

Aberdeen

Aberdeen, Mississippi —
the town's logo
incorporates bagpipes in
the top right quadrant to
symbolise its Scottish past

Aberdeen derives from the Britonnic word 'Aber' meaning 'mouth' or 'confluence'. Therefore the name originates from the position 'at the mouth of River Don' and refers to the site of the old town of Aberdeen, Scotland which was a Pictish settlement. The modern site of Aberdeen is close to the River Dee which has probably influenced the modern spelling of Aberdeen.

Aberdeen, Scotland is often called 'the Granite City' because of the grey granite stone much of the city is built of. Traditional industries included fishing and engineering but the discovery of North Sea oil in the 1960s and 70s transformed the city into the 'offshore capital' of Europe.

Throughout the world, from the United States to Hong Kong, from Australia to South Africa there are at least sixteen towns named Aberdeen.

Probably one of the first Aberdeens to be named after the Scottish city was Aberdeen, New Jersey which was settled in the seventeenth century by Scots who fled their homeland to escape religious oppression and christened their settlement New Aberdeen. However the name was not officially recognised until 1977 when the change was made from Matawan to Aberdeen following a two year campaign by the residents.

The first large group of settlers were mainly Scots Presbyterians who arrived on board the 350 ton *Henry and Francis*. Many of them were fleeing religious oppression by the Stuart kings. Another group were Covenanters who had been banished from their Highland homes to become bonded servants to George Scott, Laird of Pitlochie, Fife, to help establish an East Jersey settlement. Others were Scottish peasants who had been jailed for refusing to follow the Church of England.

Sixty of the two hundred people aboard the *Henry and Francis* died during the crossing when a violent fever swept the ship as it crossed the Atlantic in August 1685. The fever however had a silver lining as George Scott, the Laird of Pitlochie and his wife were among the dead, leaving the survivors free men and women.

But the Scottish Convenanters still had to fight for their freedom as the daughter of George Scott, Euphemia, survived the trip. She had married a passenger, Dr John Johnstone who claimed the prisoners should serve him for four years in the New World. But they refused and a court ruled that they had no obligation to do so.

Only two hundred kilometres south of Aberdeen, New Jersey lies another Aberdeen in Maryland.

The Maryland settlement began as Hall's Cross Roads in the eighteenth century, a relay point and tavern on the intersection of Old Post Road and Bush Neck Road which were built in the seventeenth century to enable farmers and planters to ship their tobacco to the overseas markets. The tavern served many travellers and even George Washington is said to have stopped there.

By the turn of the nineteenth century the settlement consisted of just a tavern, a blacksmith shop and three houses, but in the mid 1830s Aberdeen, Maryland was put on the map when the Baltimore and Port Deposit Railroad built a line through the small hamlet.

A Scot known only as Mr Winston arrived in 1835 occupying a house on the railroad right of way which became Aberdeen's first station. He became stationmaster and was allowed to name the new station after his hometown in Scotland.

With the arrival of the railroad Aberdeen became a shipping point for local agricultural products for Baltimore and Philadelphia, but today the main industries are tourism and a military base. Aberdeen Proving Ground lies adjacent to the town and is one of Maryland's largest employers. The base is used for the research and development of military hardware and munitions and is the largest employer in the county. In 1992 the base had a population of 15,000 – 3,000 more people than the town itself – and a DAILY payroll of $1million.

In 1992 to celebrate one hundred years of incorporation, the Maryland town invited the Lord Provost of Aberdeen, Scotland, William Fraser and his wife Marian to join them.

In the same year that Aberdeen, Maryland was formed, 1835, another Scot, Robert Gordon founded Aberdeen, Mississippi. Gordon was born in Minnegoff, Scotland in 1788 but emigrated to the United States with his brother, James. He lived for a while at Nashville with his brother but in 1823 at the age of thirty five he arrived at Cotton Gin Port where Aberdeen, Mississippi now stands.

Robert Gordon wore many hats. He was an Indian trader, a storekeeper and a land speculator. Gordon was trusted by the local Indian tribe, the Chickasaws, and was one of the few whites present at the signing of the Chickasaw Indian Treaty at Pontotoc on October 20th, 1832.

A provision of this treaty gave Robert Gordon a section of land to pay off debts that were owed to him by some of the so-called indigent Indians. On this land he planned the town of Aberdeen and his stock company began selling lots in 1836.

But Robert Gordon was not happy with the politics of the people living in his town so some time in the 1850s he left Mississippi to live among the Chickasaws in Indian Territory.

There was a settlement here previous to Aberdeen that was first known as Morgan's Ferry, and later as Martin's Bluff. When Gordon arrived in 1835 he began a settlement on the Tombigbee river opposite Martin's Bluff and named it Aberdeen.

In the beginning people called the town, on both sides of the river, Martin's Bluff, but Gordon's site grew so rapidly that those who did not know the new name were few and far between. Aberdeen was once the second largest city in the State of Mississppi and was the largest port on the Tombigbee River.

Aberdeen stole the trade of a number of towns to the west and north as its position on the Tombigbee was as far as steamboats could travel up river. The cotton industry thrived and the wealthy merchants and landowners built mansions in the town.

The arrival of a railroad in the 1850s diverted trade away from the port to the small railroad towns. Later the Civil War brought about a collapse of Aberdeen's cotton trade.

At one time Aberdeen was nicknamed 'Jugtown' because of its thriving whisky trade. But prohibition arrived in Aberdeen in 1901, almost twenty years before it was enforced nationwide forcing the large whisky merchants to move to Memphis, Jackson and other places in Tennessee.

In 1987 Aberdeen, Mississippi celebrated its sesquicentennial, (one hundred and fiftieth anniversary) of its incorporation in 1837. To mark the occasion a new coat of arms was adopted by the city.

It was designed in the colours of Robert Gordon's clan tartan depicting a bagpipe in one of its four corners. In another corner is a picture of Halley's Comet which is said to have been in the sky in 1836 when Gordon sold the first lots of Aberdeen and it was seen again in 1986 when the sesquicentennial celebrations began.

In 1990 the population of Aberdeen, Mississippi stood at 6,837 and currently the main industries include chemicals, plastics and bentonite clay.

Still in the United States, a city called Aberdeen is currently the third largest in the state of South Dakota. It is mainly a farming community with around 25,000 population. When they built a track though the place, the settlement was named by the Chicago, Milwaukee and Saint Paul Railroad, after the birthplace, in Scotland, of their President, Alexander Mitchell.

According to an Aberdeen, South Dakota history book, Mitchell was born the son of a farmer in 1817 in the rural town of Mill of Fortrie in Aberdeenshire, Scotland "where he grew up with his close friend Andrew Carnegie". However, many readers will know that millionaire business tycoon Andrew Carnegie was born in a weaver's cottage in Dunfermline in 1835, which would have made him four years old when Mitchell emigrated! Carnegie's parents were forced to emigrate to the United States several years later in 1848 because of a decline in handloom weaving. So it is more likely that the two. Scots became acquainted in the United States where both became involved in the railroad business.

Alexander Mitchell, although the son of a farmer, decided to read about law in an office in Aberdeen. Two years later he was working at a bank in a small village north of Aberdeen when he was asked by another Scot, George Smith, if he would help start a bank in Milwaukee, Wisconsin. He was only twenty one.

Mitchell arrived in Milwaukee in May 1839 with $50,000 of Smith's capital. He faced a major problem however – banking was illegal in Wisconsin and Mitchell faced the danger of mob violence as there were still memories of previous underhand banking deals in which many people were cheated of their cash.

But Alexander Mitchell overcame this by establishing the Wisconsin Marine & Fire Insurance Company. His banknotes which were engraved on silk paper were called 'certificates of deposit'. Mitchell eventually became the President of the Milwaukee and St Paul Railroad in 1867, and when the railroad built a line from Milwaukee to Chicago two towns were named after him – Mitchell and Aberdeen.

Aberdeen, South Dakota however, had a strong rival. Another railroad whose track crossed the Milwaukee & St Paul route at Aberdeen, refused to recognise Aberdeen as a station on the line and promoted their town, Ordway instead. They did not put Aberdeen on any of their maps, built no depot and sold no tickets for Aberdeen.

By law all trains had to stop before they crossed the Milwaukee track but many of the drivers made the stop as brief as possible. For the first year travellers to Aberdeen had to buy tickets to Ordway and when the train stopped at the crossing they would throw their baggage off the train and jump off onto the prairie.

Soon after the crossing was named Aberdeen, Mitchell's friend Andrew Carnegie founded hundreds of libraries all over the United States as gifts, all of which are named after himself – except one that is. Andrew Carnegie named the library in Aberdeen, South Dakota the Alexander Mitchell library after his friend.

In the beginning, relations were good between the town of Aberdeen, South Dakota and its namesake in Scotland. Scotsman,

Duncan McFarlane who settled in Aberdeen, South Dakota, said of the Granite City after his fourth visit in six years in 1936, "It's all right goin' over there as a tourist. The only trouble over there is it rains too much in some places. We don't get enough here and they have too much."

Communications between Aberdeen, South Dakota and its namesake in Scotland were re-established in 1992 when Alec Mayor, President of the Aberdeen Chamber of Commerce (Scotland) visited the South Dakota City.

Aberdeen in Brown County, south west of Ohio lies on the Ohio river opposite Maysville, Kentucky. It had a population of 551 during the 1950 census.

Aberdeen, Idaho lies in Bingham county in the south east of the state and had a population of almost 1,500 in 1950.

Aberdeen, North Carolina had a population of 1,603 in 1950. It was incorporated in 1893 and served as a trade centre and shipping point for tobacco and fruit.

An Aberdeen in Pennsylvania proved extremely difficult to trace. As the American telephone operator explained, "It's very small. It doesn't even have a police station or a post office."

The list of Aberdeens in the United States also includes ones in Arkansas, Kentucky, California and Washington.

In Australia there is an Aberdeen in New South Wales, which lies 70 miles north west of Newcastle and which had a population of around 1,000 in 1961.

The Hong Kong Tourist Association also made comment on the climate of their Scottish namesake. Writing a feature on Aberdeen Hong Kong, a 'fishing village' they began, "Aberdeen – the warm one on the south of Hong Kong Island, not the cold one on the east coast of Scotland." At a first glance the two towns may seem similar – both being major ports, but we are assured by the Hong Kong Tourist Association that the towns have no similarity whatsoever.

It is not just the climate that sets the two harbours apart. Whilst the Scottish harbour is full of boats servicing the North Sea oil rigs, Hong Kong's Aberdeen harbour is home to around 5,000 people who live aboard their sampans amongst the fishing fleet and the giant multi-storey floating Chinese restaurants! The Chinese name for Aberdeen, Hong Kong is Shekpaiwan.

Aberdeen, South Africa was named after the birthplace of Scots minister, Reverend Andrew Murray, who became minister of a church built on a farm at Brakkeefontein in Cape Province, around which grew the village of Aberdeen. Lying in the Aberdeen District, it was laid out in 1856 by the Dutch Reformed Church twenty miles south of the Cambedoo Mountains.

The farming community can claim to be home to the South African version of the Leaning Tower of Pisa. The massive N G Church which was built in 1907 can hold a congregation of 2,000 but its 164ft 2in steeple, the highest in South Africa, is 18 inches out of plumb.

Many of the first settlers of Aberdeen, Tasmania were Scots but the reason for the naming of the village in the city of Devonport, Tasmania is somewhat vague.

There are two possible reasons for the Scottish name of the village. It is possible that the town was named by one of its early settlers who may have come from Aberdeen, Scotland. Or it has been suggested that it was named after George Hamilton Gordon, Earl of Aberdeen, Secretary for the Colonies in 1834-35 and Prime Minister of Britain in 1852.

However John Taylor, a researcher of the Tasmanian nomenclature added, "Another possibility ties in more closely with settlement of the area by Scotsmen." He suggests that a person from the east coast of Scotland who may have known the etymology of the name may have named the Tasmania district. Whereas Aberdeen, Scotland lies at the mouth of the River Dee, the New Zealand version is situated at the mouth of the Mersey River.

Aberdeen in Saskatchewan, Canada was not named from the city of Aberdeen, Scotland itself but in honour of John Campbell Gordon, the 7th Earl of Aberdeen and 1st Marquis of Aberdeen and Temair.

And in Canada there is also a town named Balmoral in New Brunswick named after the royal residence in Aberdeenshire, Scotland as a tribute both to Scotland and to the royals.

Ayrshire

Throughout the world there are some eleven towns and cities named after the Ayrshire region of Scotland. Not all however have been named by Scots settlers.

Mount Ayr, Iowa was for example named by a visitor who simply thought that, "Ayr of Scotland was one of the prettiest names on the map!"

However the local history book *Early History of Ringgold County* claims that the town's name was chosen "in honour of Robert Burns' birthplace of Ayre, in Scotland." Unfortunately the writer seems to have been misled as to the spelling of Ayr. And of course, Robert Burns was born in Alloway, not Ayr.

The name was actually chosen by Ezra Windle, brother-in-law of one of the three land commissioners who were appointed to pick a site near to the centre of Ringgold County, Iowa, to establish a county seat in 1855.

Windle was visiting at the time and was asked to suggest a name for the yet to be developed county seat. He suggested that the seat be built on the highest area of land and that the place be called Mount Ayr.

Despite the arbitrary fashion in which the name was chosen, Mount Ayr is so proud of its Scottish title that they have even invented a rival to Scotland's Loch Ness Monster.

The Loch Ayr Monster is claimed to lurk beneath the waters of Loch Ayr, a 78 acre lake beside the town. "Like Loch Ness we have a monster, but ours is just for fun," explained Jane Lawhead, executive secretary of Mount Ayr Chamber of Commerce.

Some may say the population of Mount Ayr have gone overboard in their determination to emphasise their Scottish tradition. Tourists to the Iowa town are invited to make a telephone call from the

'Scottish telephone booth' in Mount Ayr Square. The booth is in fact an old fashioned red telephone box of the type used until recently throughout the whole of the United Kingdom.

Once a year the residents of Mount Ayr, Iowa go Scots daft when the Mount Ayr celebrations are held in the city. These include a Scottish Open Golf tournament and Scottish youth games. A regular feature of the Ayr Day's celebrations is the Scottish Highlanders, a pipe and drum band from the University of Iowa who perform with a group of Scottish dancers.

The land in which Mount Ayr lies was owned by France until 1803 when Thomas Jefferson purchased millions of acres of land in the 'Louisiana purchase'.

The Ringgold County area remained unsettled by whites until 1842 when a treaty was signed between the Government and two local Indian tribes, the Sac and Fox, which allowed whites to settle in the area the following year. In 1847 the boundaries of the county were established and named Ringgold after Major Samuel Ringgold, who was killed in the Mexican War. But there was still no county seat so steps were taken to find one.

The first attempt never really got off the ground but in 1851 following an Act passed by the Iowa General Assembly three men were appointed as commissioners to locate a position for the county seat. After finding a suitable spot the commissioners reported to the Decatur County board of commissioners that they had selected the site, marked it with a stake and named the site Urbana. However, the county had not been surveyed and the commissioners could not describe their location precisely and the stake was lost.

The third attempt to establish a county seat, as described earlier, was on April 16, 1855 when four men were appointed as commissioners to choose a site following a survey of the county. Two days later they reported back to the Decatur County judge, "We have examined the different portions of said county of Ringgold, after having been duly qualified, and have made selection of the southwest quarter of section 6, township 68 north, range 29 west, for the seat of justice of said county of Ringgold, and given it the name of Mount Ayr." The site had been chosen and two months later the first resident settled in Mount Ayr, which today has a population of around 1,796.

Another town in Iowa State carries the name of Ayrshire and it too had its title bestowed upon it in a rather unusual fashion. Ayrshire was set to be named something completely different – Godwit! – after a species of waterfowl.

Railroad companies often chose the names of the early settlements which were established as the Iron Horse pushed west. In this case the Des Moines and Fort Dodge Railway Company adopted names of waterfowl for each new town as they built the track through Iowa.

This explains the existence of such towns as Mallard, Curlew and Plover. However the residents of Godwit did not rate the name chosen for themselves and instead chose Sherlock City to honour James Sherlock, the first postmaster.

This was then changed to Silver Lake Center which still appears on the original application for a post office – but crossed out and replaced by Ayrshire.

The local history book of the Iowa town suggests two possible reasons for naming the town after the Scottish place. One suggests that it was named after a Miss Ayr who once lived in the town. Another says it was named after a "beautiful herd of Ayrshire cattle" that grazed nearby!

But the most accepted version is that the name was chosen by a Mr J C Johnson who lived just north of the town. He told the residents how the marshy rolling land of the area reminded of his home overseas. The residents, it is said, were so moved when he suggested that the town be named in honour of Ayrshire, Scotland, they changed the name for him.

There is no doubt how the town of Ayr in Queensland received its name. It was named in 1882 by the then Premier of Queensland, Sir Thomas McIllwraith after his Scottish birthplace.

There had been a settlement in Queensland's Burdekin Valley area twenty years previously, known as Wickham, but this was destroyed when the Burdekin River flooded in 1864.

The town was named Wickham to honour Captain Wickham, an explorer who travelled the coastline in the 1840s in the hope of discovering suitable ports. He gave his name to the river in the area which was later renamed Burdekin after another explorer.

Wickham was the first white to enter the region and there were few who followed for some time. James Morrill was one of the few, becoming the first settler when he was shipwrecked and drifted onto the coast on a raft. He was not Scottish, but an English sailor who was the only survivor of the ship *Peruvian*, shipwrecked on its way to China.

Morrill arrived in 1846 and lived in the area for seventeen years with the native aboriginals by which time he had almost forgotten how to speak English. However he quickly remembered when one day he strolled onto a sheep station stockyard. Knowing how trigger happy the Europeans were when confronted by an aborigine, he washed himself and shouted, "Don't shoot mates – I'm a British object!"

Up until 1901 Ayr had a rival town called Brandon which for sometime had threatened to overtake Ayr but the construction of a tramway put Ayr on the map and Brandon was out of the running.

Today Ayr has a population of over 8,000 and the early industry of sugar cane production which started in 1879 with the Burdekin Delta Sugar Company has developed the Burdekin into the sugar-growing capital of Australia.

The area produces around 900,000 tons of raw sugar each year worth around $270,000,000. One of the most spectacular sights is said to be the cane fires during mid June to mid November. However residents of Ayr have mixed reactions when it comes to the flakes of soft black ash which fall from the sky following such fires.

Nicknamed 'Burdekin Snow' the ash wreaks havoc amongst shopkeepers, car yard owners and houseproud residents – although the kids are said to love it!

Another settlement in Australia to be given an Ayrshire, Scotland placename is the City of Cessnock situated south of New South Wales and named after a castle in Ayrshire.

Cessnock too was left unsettled for many years as it lay on an escape route for convicts in the nearby penal station at Newcastle. Free settlers were not allowed into the Hunter Valley and Greater Cessnock area until 1821 when the nearby penal station was transferred to Port McQuarie. Until then the area was only traversed by escaped convicts heading towards the Hawkesbury River. Once the penal station was transferred and the Howes Valley road was opened in 1823 free settlers began arriving from the south. It was a mere bridle track that had been built by the convicts.

Among the first people to settle at Cessnock was John Campbell, pioneer and son of the Laird of Treesbank. He acquired land as early as 1826 and when his estate was put up for sale in 1853, he had already named the area Cessnock after Cessnock Castle in Ayrshire.

At first development of Cessnock was slow, losing out to Wollombi, eighteen miles west. As late as 1858 there was said to be only between seven and eleven adults living in Cessnock while Wollombi District had a population of over 1,500.

Wollombi's importance declined however when in 1870 the wheat harvest was ruined by rust. The following year Cessnock's population stood at sixty two. It was around this time that the settlement was first referred to as Cessnock and not Cessnock Estate or Cessnock Inn.

By 1901 the population had risen to 165 but Cessnock was still far smaller than its neighbouring town of Wollombi. It was the discovery of workable coal in the area in 1886 that stimulated Cessnock's growth. The first coal was struck by George Brown in the south east corner of what was Campbell's estate in 1892. During the following years several more collieries were established creating the 'land boom of 1903-23'. By 1926 Cessnock's population had exploded to 12,000.

A major pit disaster in 1923 at the Bellbird Colliery killed twenty one miners and left the residents of Greater Cessnock shocked. And matters worsened in 1929 with the onset of the 'Great Depression' which lasted a decade. Things looked up when during the years 1939-45 coalminers in the area broke all production records, but the celebrations were shortlived as in the post war years the industry declined.

Today, one of the larger industries of Greater Cessnock is the vineyards. There are a total of 4,200 acres of vineyards in Cessnock which have turned the area into a tourist attraction.

Five hundred miles south of Cessnock lies the town of Ardrossan, South Australia which, similar to its Scottish namesake, is a sea port. It is currently the largest sea port on the north east coast of St Vincent Gulf, Yorke Peninsula with a population of around 1,000.

This town was named by Governor Sir James Fergusson after his home town in Scotland. However, a writer of the Australian Ardrossan's history book may have been misinformed as it claims

Ardrossan was named after a "beautiful sea port in Ayrshire, Scotland" from whence Sir James had come! Residents of Ardrossan on the Clyde coast and its many visitors catching the Arran ferry will accept such a compliment with good grace!

In Scotland, Ardrossan and Saltcoats may be next door neighbours but their namesakes are separated by the expanse of the Pacific Ocean.

In Saskatchewan, Canada, lies the town of Saltcoats which, while not being a port itself, was named after the Ayrshire seaside town in honour of the Allan family, owners of the Allan Steamship Line who brought over many Scottish emigrants in the 1880s and 90s.

The settlement grew up around Anderson Lake, now Saltcoats Lake, which was originally named after William Anderson, the first recorded homesteader of Saltcoats who arrived in 1882, followed by his family soon after.

By 1887 several businesses had been established in the town which was originally known as Stirling, but it was soon discovered that two other communities in the Northwest Territories bore this name.

At this time a vigorous advertising campaign was underway in Eastern Canada, USA and Europe to promote Western Canada and meetings were held promising "free land and a new life in a land of milk and honey".

Unfortunately for the emigrants life was not quite so sweet. The journey over the Atlantic alone was long and hazardous. One such crossing on the Allan Ship, the *Mayflower* sailed from Scotland on March 26th, 1889.

It took almost a month for the passengers to complete their journey to the tiny settlement of Saltcoats at the end of the rail line. They arrived on April 20th, 1889. During the rough sea crossing they ran out of water and had very little food. Two infants died and had to be buried at sea.

Many of the settlers were attracted at meetings which were held in Scotland, some of which were sponsored by the Allan Steamship line. The shipping company was also involved in the building of the Manitoba Northwest Railway which ran from Portage La Prairie to Saltcoats.

In September 1888 the railroad was laid and in April the following year the first train arrived with five hundred passengers, mainly crofter families who had emigrated from Scotland under the Imperial Colonisation Board.

John A 'Scotty' MacDonald was among the first settlers to arrive at Saltcoats. He wrote in 1939, "We left our heatherclad hill and sheilings on the misty isles of the Outer Hebrides to take the long trip to our home in the New World. Following a sail of a day and a half to Glasgow, we were transferred to the Allan liner *Scandinavian* and we landed at Halifax, Nova Scotia on a Sunday afternoon. We arrived at Saltcoats on April 20, 1889."

He added, "Our homesteads were in the districts called Dunleath, Barvas, Glasgow, Stornoway, Eden and Tupper."

With the influx of residents Saltcoats grew rapidly and in 1893 a meeting was held with the intention of establishing limited self government, and the following April Saltcoats became the first official village in Northwest Territories.

At first employment opportunities were scarce in Saltcoats and many of the men walked over two hundred miles from Saltcoats to Portage to work on the harvests, stooking and threshing for a dollar a day. When the harvest season was over the men would take the train back to Saltcoats using their hard earned cash.

Today jobs are not as hard to come by in the Saskatchewan town and most of the 566 residents of Saltcoats are employed in agriculture as the town lies in one of the most productive agricultural areas in western Canada. In recent years in honour of its namesake a badge was designed for the Canadian town similar to the Scottish town's burgh seal.

Other places around the globe that carry Ayrshire names include Arrans in Ontario, Canada and Saskatchewan, Canada; Ayrs in Adams County, Nebraska, USA; in Cass County, North Dakota, USA; in Ontario, Canada which was once called Mudges Mill until renamed by Scottish settlers; and Ayr Hill which is now a district in the Virginian town of Vienna. There is also a Kilmarnock in Virginia, USA and a Saltcoats in Manitoba, Canada.

Finally in the Ayrshire connection, there is a town called Mosgiel in South Island, New Zealand. It was named by an early settler who was a leading member of the Scottish Free Church which colonised this area of New Zealand. Mosgiel was named after Mossgiel, the

Ayrshire farm where the poet Robert Burns lived for four years.

Burns was born the son of a small farmer in Alloway in Ayrshire, Scotland in 1759. Following his father's death when Robert was twenty four years old, he and his brother Gilbert rented the farm of Mossgiel but the poet dreamt of emigrating to the colonies himself.

It was while he lived at Mossgiel that he had published his first volume of poems. Titled *Poems, Chiefly in the Scottish Dialect* they were published in Kilmarnock in 1786 with the aim of raising money to allow him to emigrate to the Indies. The volume was an instant success but Burns died of rheumatic fever in 1796 at the age of just thirty seven in poverty in Dumfries.

Each June the Burns Anniversary Ride takes place in honour of the poet from Tam O' Shanter's Inn at Ayr to Brig o' Doon.

Ayr, Scotland with its sandy beaches is the most popular holiday resort on the West coast of Scotland. Ayrshire has championship golf courses including Turnberry and Royal Troon.

The Scottish Borders

The Scottish Borders is one of the most attractive areas of the country. Lying close to Scotland's southern neighbour these lands were hard fought for in the wars between England and Scotland over many centuries.

Despite the fact that only just over 100,000 people inhabit the modern day Scottish Borders, the small towns of Melrose, Roxburgh and Kelso have spawned communities throughout the world.

In the United States there are at least eleven towns named after Melrose and in total there are no less than sixteen places that have been named after this Scottish town and its famous abbey which is closely associated with Sir Walter Scott.

However there is some doubt as to how the Melrose community in South Australia came to be named after the Scottish Border town. Some believe that Melrose, South Australia was named by three Campbell brothers who camped on the site, naming it after their native town in Scotland. Although there were Campbell brothers who settled in the area, they came in fact from Glenorchy in the Highlands of Scotland, not Melrose.

Another theory was put forward in 1908 by a local resident who claimed that a man named John Armstrong, but better known as Scotty the Rinkler, named it after the abbey that he was supposed to have been born near. However it is unlikely that the Mount Remarkable Mining Company to whom the town owes its existence would give an outsider the responsibility of naming the town.

A third, more romantic, version was suggested by George Melrose, an early pastoral pioneer of South Australia who claimed that a surveyor on his property fell ill and was nursed back to health by his wife. The surveyor is said to have been so delighted that he promised to name the next town he surveyed after his benefactor.

However the most likely version is that Melrose was named by the directors of the Mount Remarkable Company after the Scottish Melrose as the sites of both towns are geographically similar.

The town was founded on the promise of rich mineral discoveries and in 1846 copper was discovered. The Australian Mining Company opened a mine in the area but it closed in 1858 after twenty thousand pounds had been invested without any return.

Melrose was proclaimed a town in 1853 making it the oldest town in the Flinders Ranges region of South Australia, named after Captain Matthew Flinders who discovered this part of the coast in 1802.

Today Melrose, Australia remains a small town with around two hundred residents who have some peculiar 'Melrose Customs'. In his book *Melrose – Child of the Mountain* author Jim Faull said, "Most tourists do not stay long enough to appreciate some of the local Melrose customs."

He added, "They would not know for instance that when a number of people use the bank together only one ever enters the banking chamber at a time. The others regardless of the weather, wait their turn outside, or in the entrance porch." He assures his readers, "The discomfort endured here at times is more acceptable than infringing on another person's financial matters."

The name Melrose comes from the Gaelic words 'maol' meaning 'bare' and 'ros' meaning 'promontory'.

The Scottish town surrounds the ruins of Melrose Abbey which was one of four great Border abbeys to be established in the reign of David I. It was built in 1136 by Cistercian monks from Rievaulx near York and became one of the wealthiest monastries in Scotland but was completely destroyed in 1385 by Richard II and replaced by another abbey in the fifteenth century.

In the 1920s excavations carried out on Melrose Abbey's ruins uncovered what is believed to be the mummified heart of Robert the Bruce whose famous victory over the English at Bannockburn in 1314 regained Scotland's freedom. The heart is encased in a cone-shaped lead container. Robert I is known to have ordered that his heart be buried at Melrose. Melrose, Scotland has a population of just over 2,000.

In North Carolina the town of Roxboro was named after Roxburgh in Scotland which lies two miles from the ruins of the town of

Roxburgh and its twelfth century castle. The name Roxburgh derives from the Old English words 'hroc' meaning 'rook' and 'burh' meaning 'fortified village'.

The town of Roxburgh was created as a Royal burgh in the early twelfth century and its castle became a popular royal residence. The marriage of Alexander II to Mary de Courcy took place in the castle, as did the birth of their son Alexander III.

Throughout the twelfth century Roxburgh was regarded as fourth in Scotland in terms of population and importance. During the next century however, the castle and town were taken over by the English, recaptured by the Scots, but taken once again to remain under English control for the next one hundred years.

It was not until the seige of 1460 that control of the town was won back by the Scots during a battle in which James II was killed by an exploding cannon. Only a few ruins and a cluster of grassy mounds now remain of the original town.

The town of Roxboro in North Carolina was aptly named as it lies near the border with Virginia which was the scene of a lengthy dispute between the two colonies who wanted the border relocated. The history of the Roxboro area in North Carolina begins with the Saponi, Tuteloand the Ocaneechi Indian tribes whose artefacts, including arrow heads and tools, have been found dating from as far back as 5000BC.

It was over 6000 years later that the first white settler entered the scene. His name was John Lederer and he traversed the area in 1670. There is no other record of another white entering the area of North Carolina until March 1728 when William Byrd was appointed to lead a group of surveyors and commissioners to draw a boundary line between Virginia and North Carolina.

This was to settle a fifty five year old dispute between the two colonies as all the settlers in North Carolina wanted the border further north to avoid the heavy taxation in the Virginia colony, while the Virginian authorities wanted the line farther south.

It was under orders from Britain that the line was placed at thirty degrees, thirty one minutes, placing Roxboro, Person County and other counties along the line which once lay in Virginia, in North Carolina.

Byrd was so impressed with the area that he applied for land grants and purchased tracts of land amounting to 26,000 acres naming it 'The Land of Eden' in 1733.

The first recorded settler of Roxboro was a Dr James Paine who settled on the present town site in the 1700s. Most of the first settlers were small farmers with holdings averaging around 150 acres.

There are several stories that are told as to the origin of the name although none can be authenticated. One of the most likely is that the name Moccasin Gap was changed at the request of a James Williamson, a wealthy landowner who had emigrated from Scotland.

Amongs the other towns named after the Scottish Roxburgh is a town of the same name on South Island, New Zealand. It isn't only the town that bears a Scottish name, as all but two of the streets in Roxburgh, New Zealand carry Scottish placenames. The small town lies in the Clutha Valley, named after the Clyde River and was originally settled by miners during the gold rushes of the1860s.

Roxburgh, which lies 150km north west of Dunedin became a borough in 1877 and today has a population of around 400. Large quantities of pip and stone fruits are grown around Roxburgh along the Clutha River.

As well as its fruit growing Roxburgh, New Zealand is noted for its massive hydro-electric dam which lies in a narrow gorge in the Clutha River valley ten miles from the village. The Roxburgh Hydro Electric power station was the largest in New Zealand when it was commissioned in 1956 with a generating capacity of 320mw.

In the south west corner of Manitoba, Canada there is a village called Reston, which derives its name from its Scottish namesake in Berwickshire. The first settlers in the area were not Scottish, but were Sioux Indians who had fled from the United States following the Custer Massacre in 1876, a large proportion of whom camped in the Pipestone valley at various points along the river.

The Sioux however could not escape the white man and only five years later white settlers began to arrive. Among them were Robert and William Bulloch who settled in the area which is now called the Lanark District, after their hometown in Lanarkshire, Scotland. The first homes at Reston were built in 1892 and 93 and by the turn of the century the population had risen to ninety nine. Reston was named by the Milliken family who had emigrated from Berwickshire, Scotland.

In 1892 the Canadian village was visited by a journalist from the *Winnipeg Free Press* who filed a glowing report. Unfortunately he got the name of the village wrong, writing, "Preston is the name of a very prosperous settlement in township 7-27."

Today Reston is an unincorporated village district with a population of around 650, its primary industries being agriculture and tourism.

There are numerous other towns scattered throughout the world carrying Scottish Borders' placenames including two Melroses in Australia.

In Canada there is a Melrose in Nova Scotia, while in the United States there are Melroses in Massachusetts, Idaho, Minnesota, Oregon, Florida, Iowa, Montana, New Mexico, Ohio and Wisconsin. Three settlements in the United States have adopted the name Melrose Park. They are in Illinois, New York and Pennsylvania.

Eildon, a town in central Victoria, Australia took its name from the Eildon Hills near Melrose in Scotland. It was originally called Eildon Weir due to the nearby dam on the Goulburn River although the name was later shortened.

In Canada the town of Jedburgh took its name from Jedburgh in the Borders of Scotland.

There are several communities called Kelso, presumably named after Kelso in Scotland due to emigrant connections. In Scotland, Kelso lies only a few miles from old Roxburgh on the confluence of the Tweed and Teviot Rivers and grew up around a medieval abbey. Although Kelso Abbey was destroyed by the Earl of Hertford in 1545 and never restored, the town was rebuilt by the end of the sixteenth century.

Sir Walter Scott spent some of his youth at Kelso grammar school where he met his classmates, brothers John and James Ballantyne, who later became his printers and publishers.

Although Kelso is a small town in the Borders of Scotland with a population in 1991 of only 5,989, it has certainly made its impression on the world map as no fewer than six other localities have taken its name.

This includes Kelso in Washington, USA which was founded in 1847 by Scottish surveyor Peter Crawford who named it after his native town in Roxburghshire. It was incorporated as a town in 1889 and later as a city in 1908, becoming the county seat of Cowlitz county, Washington in 1932, with a population of over 7,000.

The other Kelsos are situated in California, Missouri and North Dakota in the United States, Saskatchewan in Canada and in New Zealand.

Minto, a small community in the Yukon in Canada was named in honour of Gilbert John Elliot Murray Kynynmound, the 4th Earl of Minto (1845-1914), who became Governor General of Canada from 1898-1904. The earl took his title from his family seat, Minto House which is in the village of Minto near Jedburgh. Minto, New Brunswick most probably takes its name from the same person. It had a population of 3,096 in 1990.

Lastly, there are another three towns which have derived their name from Roxburgh. They are Roxboro, North Carolina; Roxburgh in the south east of South Island, New Zealand; and Roxburgh County in New South Wales.

The Scottish town has a population of 5,759 and grew up as a market town to serve the surrounding agricultural areas. Today the town still performs this function as well as a range of other industries such as electronics and plastics. In 1988 Kelso was a winner in the 'Beautiful Britain in Bloom' competition as well as the Bruce Trophy in 1988 and 1989 for the best small town in the 'Beautiful Scotland in Bloom' competitions.

The Clyde

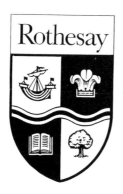

Rothesay, New Brunswick —
the crest of the town is
quartered showing the ship
that appears on the coat of
arms of Rothesay,
Scotland, another showing
the Prince of Wales
feathers whose other titles
include Duke of Rothesay

In Scotland the River Clyde rises in the depths of the Lowther Hills in the Southern Uplands and winds its way through Lanarkshire before passing through Glasgow, past Clydebank and Renfrew before becoming the wide expanse of the Firth of Clyde in which are the islands Bute, Cumbria and Arran.

Once one of the chief commercial waterways in the world, the Clyde was the home of some of the world's greatest shipbuilding firms who lined both banks between Glasgow and Greenock.

Since the end of the Second World War however, traditional shipbuilding areas along the Clyde have declined although there are places such as Govan, Port Glasgow and Greenock where shipbuilding is still carried out.

In 1759 the first of several Acts were passed for the deepening of the Clyde river so that ships could reach Glasgow and as a result the river was extensively dredged and deepened to make it navigable. But it was during the nineteenth century that the Clyde became world renowned for its concentration of shipbuilding and engineering industries.

In 1812 Henry Bell launched the *Comet* on the Clyde, which was the first commercial steamship to sail in Europe. Within the next twenty years, seventy two ships were constructed on the Clyde shipyards.

The years preceding the First World War saw a boom on the Clyde. By 1913 a staggering three quarters of a million tons were launched from shipyards on the river, but when the War ended the yards were threatened by the postwar policy of selling Germany's confiscated ships at knockdown prices.

By the 1930s the annual tonnage had dropped to 56,000. With the Second World War there was a revival in Clyde shipbuilding which lasted about ten years after the end of hostilites in 1945.

There are at least four rivers named after the Clyde, one of which is in New York State, another in Tasmania – both no doubt being named by emigrants from Scotland. The Clyde river on Baffin Island, Canada was named in 1818 by John Ross, the famous Arctic explorer.

The fourth river named after the Clyde was given the Clyde's old Celtic spelling, Clutha, when it was named in the nineteenth century by settlers of Scottish descent. The Clutha River in Otago is New Zealand's largest river, on which stands the community of Balclutha. The word 'Bal' which is common in several Scottish placenames such as Balfron and Balfour, simply means 'village' or 'settlement' so the name given to Balclutha is quite appropriate.

The town was established in the mid nineteenth century as a ferry crossing on the Clutha river. A man named Archibald Anderson had settled on the island of Inch Clutha and used his boat to ferry travellers heading south.

It was around this time that Balclutha's first white settlers arrived. They were the McNeil family whose clan had emigrated from their ancestral home, Kisimul Castle on the island of Barra. Descendants of the McNeils who had arrived at Dunedin on 26th December 1849 met at Balclutha in 1989 to celebrate the anniversary of the arrival of their forebears. Street names in Balclutha include Clyde Street, Edinburgh Place, Glasgow Street, Renfrew Street, Paisley Street, Ayr Street and Lanark Street. The population of the Clutha district is now over 19,000 whereas Balclutha has around 4,300 residents. Balclutha is the centre for a rural farming area and is also a tourist centre offering outdoor activities such as bush walks, sea coasts and beaches, hunting and fishing.

Rothesay, New Brunswick was named after the town of Rothesay which is the capital of the island of Bute in the Firth of Clyde, Scotland. The Scottish town was named back in the thirteenth century. Rothesay means Roderick's island, and was named when Rudri MacDonald was given the Isle of Bute by King Hakon of Norway.

Similar to the Scottish Clyde area, Rothesay, New Brunswick was a thriving shipbuilding region for some time. The Canadian town was established in the late eighteenth century when the area at the junction of the Kennebecasis River and the Bay of Fundy was surveyed for settlement. Many Loyalist settlers who had fled from their settlements in America arrived in the area following the American Civil War. At the same time the British government were encouraging emigration to Canada.

At one time the village of Rothesay was named Kennebecasis after the river which was given its name by the Indians who lived there. The name change took place in 1860 when the Prince of Wales made a stop at the settlement whilst on his way from Fredericton to Saint John on the newly built railway line.

The villagers, having failed to agree on a suitable name for the village and its station on a number of occasions, finally accepted a proposal that the name be changed to Rothesay to honour the Prince who also held the title Duke of Rothesay. Rothesay's town crest features in one quarter the Prince of Wales feathers. Another contains the ship which appears on the coat of arms of the Scottish burgh.

In the mid nineteenth century Rothesay, New Brunswick became an important shipbuilding community with its abundance of wood and position on the Kennebecasis River. The first shipyard was established in 1833 by Benjamin Appleby, which produced over ninety ships in its twenty four year existence.

Such was the quality of the wood in the area that the North American and New Brunswick shipbuilding companies were soon overtaking the British industry market in producing ships suited for service in the whaling fleets.

But the prosperity of the shipyards did not last. With new technology sail was replaced by steam and iron hulls replaced the wooden type. Although there was a small revival in the late nineteenth century the shipbuilding industry of Rothesay was finished and nothing ever really took its place.

A book published by the Rothesay Area Heritage Trust says, "There are no businesses, stores or outlets in Rothesay. There are also few pavements and those that do exist are 'frowned upon'." The New Brunswick town has changed so little over the years that the local guidebook on the town claims that visitors to Rothesay may feel like they are stepping back in time.

Such is the desire to retain the traditional character of the town that when a new resident built a modern house in Rothesay he was accused of "sinning against the Holy Ghost!" One homeowner was so concerned about preserving a young tree that he built an extension to his house around the tree so that it was growing through the building. As the tree grew larger the house had to be remade to accommodate it!

Another of Rothesay's architects, John A Monroe, had a more macabre claim to fame. The enterprising gentleman invented a gallows that jerked the condemned person upwards instead of letting them drop. Unfortunately for Mr Monroe his gallows worked – for he ended up personally trying out his invention when he was found guilty of the murder of his mistress and son in 1869. The judge only thought it fit that the invention be tested out on its creator! It was noticed after John Monroe was hanged that the majority of the homes he had built had been decorated with wood carved to resemble rope!

Another Canadian settlement is the village of Ailsa Craig in Ontario which takes its name from the rocky islet in the Firth of Clyde which lies off the Ayrshire coast opposite Girvan in Scotland. The village in Ontario was first called Craig's Station when it was settled in 1835 by David Craig, an emigrant from Ayrshire, Scotland. But it was discovered that there was another settlement with the same name so it was changed to Ailsa Craig after the rock which David Craig remembered seeing from his home in Scotland as a young boy.

David Craig was an engineer who had spent some time in Cuba where he constructed engines for use on the sugar plantations before arriving in the Middlesex County area of Canada in 1835. Prior to this, the area where Ailsa Craig now stands, was inhabited by Indians. The only whites to enter the area were the occasional traders in search of furs which could be obtained from the Indians in exchange for beads and trinkets.

But David Craig befriended the Indians and at one time had 120 of them camping on his land. The wild animals were a bigger risk to David and his wife as wolves, wild cats and bears wandered in the nearby forest.

David Craig had purchased his land from the Canada Company who were established in London, England in 1826. They had bought almost two and a half million acres of land from the Province of Upper Canada. When David arrived with his wife and an Irishman named Risk, he made a clearing in the forest for their home.

Their home was so remote that David and his wife were required to walk a distance of 40km to the nearest shop – a trip that had to be made on numerous occasions to buy necessities such as dry goods, boots and shoes.

The settlement of Ailsa Craig did not begin to grow until 1858 when the Grand Trunk Railway built a line between Toronto and Sarnia. Settlements sprang up along the line, Ailsa Craig being one of them as David Craig surveyed and sold lots to the incoming settlers.

Among the early pastimes of the Ontario community was ice skating and curling. After hearing that Ailsa Craig in Scotland provides the best material for curling stones the Canadian curlers placed orders to have their curling stones made with granite from the original Ailsa Craig. The stones were made in Mauchline, Ayrshire and shipped across the Atlantic. Although the village of Ailsa Craig is small with only around 900 inhabitants it is proclaimed to be known worldwide for its annual turtle races.

There are two towns in the United States that have been named Dunbarton after the Scottish Clydeside town of Dumbarton or the county of Dunbartonshire.

Dumbarton derives its name from the Gaelic words 'Dun' meaning hill or fortress and 'Breatann' meaning of the Britons – thus the name means 'hill or fortress of the Britons'. The town was the ancient capital of the Britons in Strathclyde and has one of the longest histories in the UK. Dumbarton Rock, a 240ft rock of basalt has been fortified from at least the fifth century.

It was created a royal burgh in 1222 and during the fifteenth century it rivalled Glasgow and Rutherglen as a market town, becoming the county town of Dunbartonshire. Shipbuilding began in the eighteenth century and by the mid nineteenth century the town boasted five shipyards including William Denny and Brothers who built the infamous *Cutty Sark*. Today shipbuilding and engineering has been replaced by distilling and warehousing.

The Dunbarton in South Carolina, which had a population of 262 in 1950, was taken over by the US Atomic Energy Commission for its Savannah River plant which works with hydrogen bomb materials.

However Dunbarton, New Hampshire is no ghost town – although it does have several ghost stories, and an old house for several years was known as 'the haunted house'. The Ordaway House which stood in a 'lonely hollow' according to the local history book, was feared by the locals. Loud noises were often heard coming from the empty building. One brave resident who decided to investigate found no ghost – but instead a trapped bull! Apparently the bull had wandered into the kitchen through an open door but when the wind blew the door shut the bull became a prisoner. It had eaten pieces of the woodwork and when discovered was almost starved to death.

Another eerie tale talks about a railroad engineer who was a resident of the town. One day whilst waiting on the siding for a train, he seemed to see a vision of his dead father through the cab window of the engine. At first he did not pay attention but the vision stayed there and seemed to motion him to look up the rail track. On doing so he saw a train heading directly towards him – the vision almost certainly saved his life.

Dunbarton, New Hampshire was settled by the Stark family who had emigrated from Dumbarton, Scotland. One member of the family was General John Stark, regarded as a famous Revolutionary War hero.

His son was Celeb Stark. So determined was he to follow in his father's footsteps, that at the age of just fifteen he ran away from home to join his father at the battle of Bunker Hill. Celeb is pictured on the town crest on horseback, heading to Bunker Hill, with two of his friends chasing after him – Caleb apparently forgot to put on some articles of his clothing but nobody knows if they ever caught up with him.

At one time the New Hampshire village was named Starkstown when the land was granted to Archibald Stark in 1748. However the name was changed to Dunbarton when the settlement was incorporated in 1765. To mark the town's bicentennial on August 7th, 1965, John Campbell, the Provost of the Royal Burgh of Dumbarton, Scotland presented the residents of Dunbarton, New Hampshire with a three volume series *The Book of Dunbartonshire*.

Dunbarton now has a population of around 1,700 and is described as a "small town, commonly referred to as a bedroom community" by one of the town's selectmen who added, "we have no serious industry, nor do we desire any."

One odd feature of the town today which has carried on for many years is that most of the town's services are provided by residents who volunteer their time. This practice "emanates from both a desire to lend a hand and to help keep the tax rate low." Services such as recycling, school aids, even fire and police protection are largely volunteer efforts.

Dunbarton's chief of police, Don Andrews admitted, "Law enforcement is no longer a simple process governed by common sense, courage and diligence. Every action an officer makes has to be capable of passing through the courts." For this reason the success of the Dunbarton police service is graded on the lose/win record in the courts. Police volunteers regularly receive training from the New Hampshire State Police and State Police Standards and Training instructors – even the FBI.

But Don Andrews points out that even though the training is very beneficial, one of the most important factors in police work is the residents of Dunbarton. He advises the townsfolk, "Anyone noticing something wrong or strange vehicles or persons should notify the police with as good a description as possible."

The only other town to be discovered during my research to be named after a namesake in the Clyde region of Scotland is the tiny community of Greenock, Ontario in Canada.

Dumfriesshire

Dumfries, Virginia — the
ceremonial seal of the
Virginia town contains two
thistles to emphasise the
Scottish origins

I t is not surprising that Dumfries and other towns in south west
Scotland should have spawned other namesakes. After all the
area along the Solway Firth was a jumping off point for trade
with the New World on the other side of the Atlantic.

Dumfries, the largest town in the region, prospered during the
nineteenth century with its port being the busiest in the south of
Scotland with access to England and America.

Dumfries derives from the Gaelic words 'Dun' meaning 'hill' and
'phreas' meaning 'copse'. Some dispute this however, claiming that
the 'fries' part of the name refers to a settlement made by the Frisians
although there is no evidence to back this.

The Scottish town is often referred to as the 'Queen of the South'
due to its close proximity to England, a title which is given to its
main football club.

The writer Defoe described Dumfries as "a prosperous town of
merchant adventurers". He also described the castle as "very

magnificent" but unfortunately this was demolished soon after his visit to make way for a church in 1727.

Dumfriesshire is southern Scotland's largest county with a population of almost 90,000, while the town's population stood at 32,136 in 1991.

There are towns named Dumfries in the United States and another settlement called North Dumfries in Canada.

Like its namesake, Dumfries, Virginia was once a busy port, first settled by wealthy tobacco merchants and around 3,500 rebel prisoners who were exiled there following the Jacobite defeat at Culloden in 1746. These early settlers sent home descriptions of freedom, potential and a land where, after a short indenture period, a man could become king of his own domain.

During the mid eighteenth century tobacco warehouses lined the wharf of Dumfries harbour in Virginia. Tobacco inspectors were stationed at all major points of shipping to protect the British Crown's interest and to ensure that the commodity was shipped to Britain rather to other countries.

Nearly all of the storekeepers in Dumfries were of Scottish ancestry and were factors of, or represented, tobacco barons back in Glasgow. By 1725 tobacco plantations lined the bank of the Potomac River, with Dumfries at Quantico Creek offering the best harbour for trading.

In 1763 the town of Dumfries peaked in size and importance when the total tonnage of imports and exports matched that of New York and Philadelphia. Most of the land in the watershed of Quantico Creek was under cultivation but it was this that led to the town's downfall. The large scale cultivation caused soil erosion and topsoil was carried downriver and settled at the mouth of Dumfries harbour. After just fifteen years the port became unnavigable for larger ships and tobacco had to be transported from the wharfs to the ships by small craft, making Dumfries uncompetitive compared to other major ports. By the end of the eighteenth century many of the merchants had moved to rival ports.

In the 1890s the town enjoyed partial recovery when an iron pyrite mine opened up in the Quantico Creek area and remained open until the 1960s. Today Dumfries, Virginia is a small incorporated town with a population of 5,000, in Prince William County, one mile west of the Potomac River, thirty five miles south of Washington DC.

Two towns have adopted the name of Gretna after the famous village situated on the Scottish border with England which is famous for its runaway marriages.

Gretna lies near the Solway Firth in Scotland and the name is said to derive from the Old English words 'greot' which means 'gravel' and 'hohl' meaning 'hollow'. For a long time Gretna was regarded as 'debatable land' as the Anglo Scottish border was often interpreted as following the Esk or Sark river.

It wasn't until 1707 that the Act of Union finally settled the argument and Gretna and its adjacent village of Gretna Green ceased to provide a safe haven for smugglers. However the smuggling of whisky carried on until the nineteenth century as the duties in England were heavier than those in Scotland.

A tightening of marriage laws in England in 1754 gave Gretna a sweeter reputation when eloping English couples were enticed to the village just over the border in Scotland where the laws were less stringent and where marriages before two witnesses were allowed without clerical involvement. Even after law changes in Scotland couples were still attracted to the small Scottish town as the age when a young person could be married without requiring their parent's consent remained lower than in England.

Similar circumstances led to the village of Gretna, Louisiana choosing the name for the town as an early justice of the peace used to perform marriages twenty four hours a day without the need for a legal certificate. In much the same manner as eloping couples would cross the border to Scotland's Gretna Green, couples would cross the Mississippi river to be married in its sister city in Louisiana.

The first settler in the area was Jean Baptiste Destraham who received a land grant in 1721 in what was to become the largest city on the west bank of the Mississippi river south of St Louis. The settlement was first called Mechanikham but when the justice of the peace began performing marriage ceremonies day and night without marriage certificates the name was changed to Gretna. Later more land was purchased by the St Mary's Market Steam Ferry Company who developed New Gretna.

It wasn't only the Scots who settled this region of Louisiana. In the 1770s French officials recruited many settlers from the Rhine region of Germany under false pretences. They told stories of the abundance of gold and silver and lush farmland.

In 1838 the establishment of the ferry service improved access and development of Gretna and by 1880 the population had reached over 5,000. However it was not until 1913 that Gretna, Louisiana was declared a village. Only three months later the City of Gretna was proclaimed in the combination of the settlements of McDonoghville, Mechanikham and Gretna. The population of Gretna, Louisiana currently stands at 17,208 (1991), with industries ranging from manufacturing cottonseed oil and asbestos to petroleum products.

The town has had its share of famous residents down the years. Baseball player, Mel Ott who was the youngest ever major league baseball player, signing for the New York Giants at the age of just sixteen, was born in Gretna in 1909. He is named in baseball's 'Hall of Fame' having made 511 home runs, a national league record when he retired.

Other famous residents include Lash LaRue, a popular cowboy movie star of the 40s and 50s; Robert Emmet Kennedy, the musician, author and folklorist; and Frankie Ford, a rock 'n roll pianist.

Although there are no formal connections between the Scottish and Lousiana Gretnas, Ronnie C Harris the Mayor of Gretna, Louisiana said, "Occasionally we have residents from our community visit Gretna Green and bring momentos of our city to the Registrar."

Another Gretna was named due to similarities between itself and its namesake in Scotland. The town in Manitoba, Canada was a former port of entry on the Manitoba-North Dakota border and was named by the Canadian Pacific Railway in 1883 after the Scottish town which is similarly situated on the border with England.

In Scotland the village of Annan is situated between Gretna and Dumfries near the mouth of the River Annan and has been a Royal Burgh since James V was on the throne (1512-42). Annan possibly means 'swift river' deriving from the word 'an' which commonly ends the names of Celtic rivers.

At one point the Scottish town was a major port and was a centre for handloom weaving probably suffering greatly during the demise of the weaving industry.

In the past the town has been associated with Robert the Bruce who is said to have resided here before moving to Lochmaben. The

Brus Stone, which carried an inscription possibly referring to Robert the Bruce was removed from Annan in the nineteenth century. It was rediscovered in Devon, England and returned in 1925.

Thomas Bladlock, the blind poet who was reputed to have dissuaded Robert Burns from emigrating was born in Annan.

Today Annan, Scotland has a population of alomost 9,000.

Several places have been named after Annan and its river. Among them is the village of New Annan on the Northumbrian Strait in Nova Scotia, Canada. The first settler in the area was John Oliver Bell, his wife Ann Irving and their children, who left their home in Annan, Scotland and settled in Nova Scotia in 1806. In 1812 John received a land grant of 450 acres and being the first settler, named his settlement after his home town in Scotland. During the next few years several other families joined John from Annan, Scotland, cleared the land for farms and built mills on the Bell River, named after founder, John Bell.

Soon a thriving community of Scots Presbyterians was established and the New Annan area became known as West New Annan, Central New Annan, East New Annan and Annandale. Over the next century the area lost many of its people due to migration to the Boston area and Western Canada. Today New Annan is a rural area with no real industry.

Similarly on Prince Edward Island, off the east coast of Nova Scotia, there is a settlement named New Annan which was named in the 1820s by an emigrant from Annan, Scotland. Nearby there is Annandale which was named by James Johnstone, a Scot who arrived here from Dumfriesshire, Scotland in the 1840s.

Other towns carrying south west of Scotland placenames include Annan, Ontario; Dumfries, Quebec; Stranraer, Saskatchwan; North Dumfries, Ontario; and Nith River in Ontario, all Canada.

In the USA there is a town, county and tunnel named after the Scottish community of Moffat. The county in the extreme north west of Colorado had a population of almost 6,000 in 1950 whilst the town of Moffat in Saguache county in southern Colorado had a population of just over 100.

In north central Colorado the Moffat Tunnel is 6.4 miles long at an altitude of 9,000ft. It was first used to carry water to Denver when it was built between 1823 and 1827. The following year a second tunnel was made measuring twenty four feet by eighteen feet and was used by the railroad.

In Scotland Moffat is near the head of Annandale. Moffat was once on the main road from Scotland to England. However the town is now bypassed by the M74. The Scottish town achieved burgh status in 1648, a century before the town's sulphur springs became fashionable for Scottish notables. When the age of the railways arrived the town suffered as other, more remote springs such as Bridge of Allan and Strathpeffer became accessible.

Dundee

D undee, one of Scotland's four main cities with 159,000 residents, lies on the north shore of the Firth of Tay on the country's eastern seaboard. The seaport can trace its origins back to when it was the site of a Mesolithic settlement around 2,000 BC.

The name Dundee probably comes from a much later Iron Age fort which was called Dun Diagh built on Dundee Law, the hill which rises 182 metres above the city.

The first mention of a more substantial settlement at Dundee was in 1054, and the town was later granted burgh status in 1190 by William the Lion.

Dundee once boasted a castle which was built around 1290, but unfortunately it was demolished after only around twenty five years. It is believed to have stood on an igneous rock intrusion that stood twenty seven metres above the river, where the present day cathedral now stands.

By 1500 the population of Dundee had grown to almost 7,000 and the town was actively exporting woollen cloth to the Baltic in exchange for pitch, tar, iron and copper from Sweden. This trade came to an end in the mid seventeenth century due to attacks by the English army, in particular General Monk who captured sixty ships in 1651.

In 1690 Dundee again established itself in the manufacturing and trading of linen cloth. In the nineteenth century the city earned the nickname Jute-opolis due to the cheap fibre that replaced flax during the middle of the century. The flourishing textile industry brought with it an influx of citizens. The population increased by fifty per cent between 1821-31 and by another third again between 1831-41 including around 8,000 Irish immigrants.

The population movement was not all one way. At the same time as people arrived others were leaving to settle throughout the world which led to the naming of at least twenty places after the Scots city in the United States, Canada, Australia and South Africa.

While Dundee, Scotland earned the name Jute-opolis, a town of the same name in South Africa was nicknamed 'Coal-opolis' due to the large concentration of coal mines in the area. Dundee in Natal, South Africa was first settled in 1855 by Thomas Smith, a Scotsman who bought 3,000 acres of land and created a farm which he named Dundee after the Scots city. Thomas was followed by his brother Peter who brought his wife Ann and their children.

Thomas and Peter Smith had grown up on Mole Hill Farm in Forfarshire, near Dundee, Scotland and were the sons of Thomas Smith and Mary Paterson. Thomas Smith left his home in the 1850s and spent five years on the Australian gold fields before emigrating to northern Natal where he became a farmer.

When Peter Smith arrived in Natal in 1859 the region was suffering from economic recession and the government had ceased to grant land to immigrants. So Peter and fellow traveller, William Duff, leased a farm. However this proved unsuccessful and they soon had to earn money by felling trees in the Drakensberg escarpment. They were paid for this in cattle and returned to farming in 1864.

That year Thomas persuaded his brother to join him at Dundee and while Peter took over the farming duties, Thomas continued with building contracting. Shortly after moving to Dundee Peter discovered coal only five hundred metres from the homestead on Talana hillside. He began mining and by 1878 was employing Cornish miners. He sold his coal at the market in Pietermaritzburg bringing his family a fortune.

A small settlement of thatched cottages grew up around the Steenkoolstroom valley as the coal mining operations expanded. In June 1879 the settlement enjoyed a boom when the British army made the valley their headquarters for the second invasion of Zululand.

Peter Smith brought out a mining engineer named McConnachie from Dundee, Scotland to develop further coal deposits and the first shaft was sunk where the present day city now stands.

At that time coal was brought to the surface in buckets attached to rope pulled by a pair of oxen. This mine continued to operate until 1935. For the few months during the Anglo-Zulu War in 1879 the settlement was a hive of activity but when the soldiers departed the settlement again became a backwater.

During this time Peter Smith recognised the valley's potential as a town site and in 1882 Peter, his son William, his son-in-law and friend established the town of Dundee on 1,000 acres of his farm. As a result of the coal boom the tiny settlement attracted many settlers and due to the massive number of coal mines in and around Dundee, by the turn of the century it had earned the nickname of Coal-opolis.

In 1899 the residents of Dundee, Natal were to witness a second war when the town was occupied by the Boers and renamed Meyersdorp. However the war lasted only seven months after which the name reverted back to Dundee.

Today Dundee is a tourist centre and popular stop-off point for visitors of the four Zulu and Boer battlefields, Blood River, Isandlwana, Rorkes Drift and Talana which are all less then forty five minutes drive from Dundee.

Dundee is also home to the Talana Museum which is the only museum in South Africa on a battlefield where the buildings from the time of the battle still stand. The museum covers twenty acres and includes two British forts and the remains of the Boer and British gun emplacements and the stone cairn which marks the spot where General Penn Symons fell mortally wounded. The town now has around 20,000 residents.

While Dundee, South Africa is famous for its proximity to the battlefields of the Anglo-Zulu War, in 1879 a town of the same name in Michigan was to be established near the site of the battle of the Raisin River.

The first settler of the Michigan community of Dundee arrived several years after the battle however. He was Riley Ingersoll who arrived from New York State in 1824, building a log house where the village now stands. Dundee was not the first choice of name for the Michigan settlement. It had previously been called Winfield by the first postmaster, John Montgomery when he established a post office in 1834. The name was changed to Dundee in 1836.

However there are two possibilities as to who named the town. One version written by John McClelland Bulkley in his book *History of Monroe County* claims that a man named Alonzo Curtis took over the position of postmaster, naming it Dundee. This version is repeated by Walter Romig in *Michegan Placenames* which also states that Curtis named the town site after the home of his forebears. However the Monroe County Historical Society claim that the town was named by an Ebneezer Dustin after his hometown in Scotland.

Up until 1807 the Dundee area was not open to settlement but in this year Thomas Jefferson commissioned William Hull, governor of the territory to negotiate a treaty with the local Indian tribes to release the entire eastern half of Michegan from Indian title. The treaty was drawn up on November 17th, 1807, part of which set aside Dundee Township as an Indian reservation. Further treaties saw the Indians forfeit all of their land except a half section given to a Potawatomi chief.

Before the town was given the name of Winfield the area was called River Raisin, named by two French missionaries who travelled along Lake Erie and up river in seventeenth century. They noted the wild grapes growing around the trees on the banks of the river. The Indians called the river 'Nummaseppe' or 'river of sturgeon' due to the mass of fish that entered the stream.

The local Indian tribes included Chippewa, Ottawa, Potawatomi and Wyandotte. These were mainly peaceful people and were not the Indians involved in the notorious Battle of the River Raisin at Frenchtown in 1813. It was the eastern Iroquois who fought the British encouraged by promises of $8 bounty for every American scalp taken.

Almost 2,000 kilometres to the west of the Michegan settlement is Dundee Oregon which lies in the Willamette Valley area of Yamhill county. Dundee, Oregon was named by William Reid who was born in Glasgow, Scotland in 1842. His father was manager of the Glasgow and Southwestern Railway.

William graduated from Glasgow University in law which enabled him to practise with Alex Douglas of Dundee, Scotland. While at Dundee he met Mrs Lincoln, the widow of Abraham Lincoln and performed some literary service for her which she gave in return the appointment of United States Vice-Consul at Dundee, a position he held between 1869 and 1874.

In 1878 William Reid devised a system of narrow gauge railroads which he proposed to build with Scots capital under the name of the Oregonian Railway Company. In order to achieve this he had to see the passing of a law which entitled foreign corporations to build railroads in the United States with the same powers as domestic corporations.

In 1881 the railroad built a large hotel-depot on land purchased by Reid and named it 'Dundee Junction' after the Scottish home of the mother company, Dundee in Scotland.

William Reid and the Pacific Real Estate and Investment Company, who owned the town site of Dundee, offered the land for sale allowing purchasers time to get better established before payment was made and the town began to flourish. However when Southern Pacific took over ownership of the railroad, the track was changed, the machine shops moved to nearby Portland and the hotel was demolished.

It was around this time that Yamhill county became a centre for growing all types of fruit and before long Dundee claimed to have the largest prune orchard in the United States. Dundee, Oregon had a population of 208 in 1950 and remains a centre for the growing of prunes, walnuts and filberts.

West of the Oregon community lies a town named New Dundee, Ontario which was settled in 1830 by John Millar, one of three Millar brothers who emigrated to Canada from Dundee, Scotland. John Millar is believed to have built the settlement with his brother Frederick on land given to them by the Canada Land Company in March 1830.

The town has a rather unusual claim to fame. One of the town's houses has on display a lightbulb which is claimed to have burned for more than forty years! The 75 watt bulb was in daily use from 1917 until 1957 burning approximately 18,000 hours – most bulbs guarantee to burn just 1,500 hours. The owner of the bulb is said to have been offered a carton of new bulbs from Westinghouse, the electrics company, in exchange for his burnt-out bulb, but he refused.

Today New Dundee, Ontario has around 1,200 residents and is part of Wilmot Township. One of the major employers of the community is the New Dundee Creamery which was established in 1908. The town is surrounded by rich agricultural land and many farms, some of which still bear the names of turn-of-the-century settlers.

In the United States the town of Dundee, Mississippi was settled in 1884 and named Carnsville after Captain Carnsville. The name was changed three years later when the town was incorporated as the Post Office objected to the name and changed it to Dundee. They claimed the name Carnsville was too similar to other town names! Dundee, Mississippi is currently a small unincorporated town with a population of between fifty and sixty residents.

Amongst the other places named after Dundee, Scotland is the settlement of the same name in New South Wales, Australia situated near the border with Queensland. Other Dundees include one in Polk County, Florida; another in Kane County, Illinois; Dundee, Indiana; one in Delaware County, Iowa; in Yates County, New York; Yamhill County, Oregon; Archer County, Texas and Dundee, Wisconsin.

In Canada there is a settlement called Dundee in Quebec and a Dundee Bight situated in the Parry Islands off the north east coast of Canada.

Finally there is also the uninhabited Dundee Island in Antartica which was discovered in 1893 by Scottish explorer Thomas Robertson.

Edinburgh

E dinburgh, Scotland is referred to as Dun Edin, the hillfort of Edin, as far back as the sixth century. The name derives from the Gaelic words 'dun' meaning 'hill, fortress or mound' and 'aodann' meaning 'slope'.

Settlement of the area began much earlier however, about 3000 BC, when stone-using hunters arrived followed around two thousand years later by primitive farmers. Next to follow were the Celts who had been driven north by lowland European tribes who invaded England. The Romans arrived too, in 78AD.

Edinburgh was created a Royal Burgh in the twelfth century after David I founded Holyrood Abbey in 1128. The settlement of Edinburgh, Scotland grew up around the Castle Hill and by 1376, records show that there were around 2,000 people living in the burgh, with around 400 households. Today the population stands at 410,910.

Edinburgh Castle which lies on one of the five extinct volcanoes of the area, was never successfully stormed, and throughout its 1300 year history has served as a palace, fort, prison, garrison, armoury, arsenal and today holds the Scottish crown jewels. Some of the present castle building dates back to the fourteenth century when David II returned from England and built 'David's Tower', a sixty foot high tower to protect the castle's east side.

More than 1.2 million tourists from countries throughout the world visit Edinburgh Castle every year. The three week Edinburgh Festival including the Military Tatoo held each August on the Castle Esplanade is world famous.

There are over twenty settlements named after Scotland's capital city but only three bear the actual name of Edinburgh. Most are derivations of the spelling of Edinburgh but two bear the old Celtic name, Dunedin. This name bears so little resemblance to Edinburgh that some residents of Dunedin, Florida do not realise that their city is named after the Scots capital.

In a letter the Mayor of the City of Dunedin, Florida explained that the name Dunedin was not intended to honour Edinburgh in particular, but was a combination of two names, Dundee and Edinburgh, to remember the homes of two early pioneers.

But early records of the town show that both men, J O Douglas and James Summerville, came from Edinburgh, Scotland and did in fact name the town after the Scots capital. They arrived at the site where Dunedin now stands in 1872 and recognised the need for a post office but realised that before a settlement could have a post office it required a name. To decide on the name they conducted a survey amongst the townsfolk giving them two choices – Jonesboro or Dunedin, the latter winning by an overwhelming majority.

The Florida city celebrates its Scottish roots by hosting a Highland Games and Festival every spring featuring 'a famous bagpipe highlander band'. The town is a Mecca for pipes and pipers and is now a winter resort and fishing centre with a population of over 34,000.

Not to be outdone is the City of Dunedin in New Zealand which is the only other Dunedin in the world, apart from a small district in Toronto. During the planning stages the settlement was known as New Edinburgh but it was felt that too many settlemnets in North America had been named New this and New that, so the more historic and romantic version was chosen. To reinforce the New Zealand city's Scottish origins, the planners named many of the streets after those in Edinburgh, Scotland. These include Princes, George, Castle and St Andrew and at the centre of the new settlement was the Octagon, encircled by Moray Place. Other Scottish placenames within the city of Dunedin boundary include Leith Valley, Helensburgh, Musselburgh, Corstorphine, Burnside and St Kilda.

Dunedin, New Zealand is described as the 'Edinburgh of the South' although one tourist leaflet claims, "Dunedin is nothing like the Scots capital except for the street names. Dunedin is hillier, smaller, closer to the sea and has a better climate than Edinburgh!" Yet the town was founded by Scots settlers in 1848 who named it after the Scots capital because the area reminded them of their homeland!

Robert Burns statue in Dunedin, New Zealand
Courtesy Neville Peat, photographer & author *Dunedin – a Portrait*
and Hyndman Publishing, New Zealand

Anyone who has walked up the Royal Mile to Edinburgh Castle
or The Mound would disagree about the alleged lack of contours.
And of course Leith, which is part of Edinburgh, is a port. However
there can be no argument about the climate.

Visitors to the New Zealand city may be forgiven for thinking that
they have arrived in a Scots town. Apart form the familiar street
names, I am told the shops stock haggis, kilts and Scottish
confectionery.

Golf courses, pipe bands and the Robert Burns statue in the city
may also disorientate any visitors to the area, but that's not all.
Dunedin hosts regular haggis ceremonies, Scottish dinner and
entertainment nights as well as Scottish Week, which is an annual
event for the Dunedinites. It also claims to produce "the finest range
of malts and whiskeys in New Zealand", in the country's only
distillery. Perhaps though, someone should point out to our New
Zealand cousins that Scotch whisky is spelt without an 'e'.

In the 150 years since Scots settled Dunedin they have certainly
left their mark on the city. But they were not the first settlers. Maori
explorers began arriving in the area surrounding Dunedin from
1100AD and by the time the Scots arrived the area was rich in Maori
history. Whalers later arrived in the 1820s, many of whom
intermarried with the local Maori tribe, the Otakou.

The first Scots to arrive were Captain Cargill and Reverend Tom
Burns who established a Free Church settlement in 1848. The
Reverend Thomas Burns was the nephew of Scotland's national bard,
Robert Burns. A bronze statue of Robert Burns overlooks the Octagon
as a permanent reminder of the city's Scottish past. The settlement
was boosted in the 1860s when major gold discoveries in the Otago
region sparked off the gold rush and prospectors from around the
world flooded into New Zealand to seek their fortune.

Dunedin rapidly became New Zealand's largest and wealthiest
city with a host of grand buildings, many of which survive today. The
population now stands at 118,000 and Dunedin is New Zealand's
largest city in terms of area, covering 3,350 km^2. In 1940, to mark the
centenary of the signing of the Treaty of Waitanga a memorial was
built on nearby Signal Hill, a volcanic peak overlooking Dunedin.
The lookout incorporates a piece of rock from Edinburgh Castle in
Scotland. Since 1974 Dunedin has kept in touch with its sister city,

Edinburgh, Scotland through a twinning link which has been established between the two towns.

Somewhat smaller is Edinburgh, the only settlement on the tiny island of Tristan Da Cunha in the south Atlantic Ocean, situated halfway between Cape Town and Buenos Aires. It is one of the few settlements in which the name of Edinburgh has not been altered. It was named after Prince Alfred, Duke of Edinburgh who agreed that his title could be used when he visited the island in 1867.

Disasters, shipwrecks and volcanic activity have all made life difficult for the residents of Edinburgh which is situated on the side of a spectacular volcanic cone which towers 6,760 feet above sea level. In the beginning many of the people to live on the island were the survivors of shipwrecks in the Tristan waters who remained on the island after their boats struck rocks.

The first person to settle was Thomas Currie who was one of three men to have landed from an American ship in 1810. Currie was the only one to stay on the island till his death. He was followed by three members of the British garrison, which arrived in 1816. Although the garrison was withdrawn the following year the families remained on the island and one of these men, William Glass, a Scot, is recognised as the founder of the community.

In 1827 ten emigrants arrived from St Helena increasing the population to twenty four. By 1885, the population had increased to 107 and the inhabitants prospered as ships bound for India and the Far East bartered with the locals for fresh produce and water. These were usually exchanged for sugar, flour, tea and clothing.

Between the years of 1817 and 1885 there were seventeen shipwrecks in the waters surrounding Tristan, many of the survivors of which stayed on the island for a period. One shipwreck in particular was devastating to the islanders. It happened in 1885 when a local ship was sunk, containing fifteen men, as it traded with a passing vessel. Some islanders never fully recovered from the shock and in the following years thirty four inhabitants emigrated to South Africa. This left only sixty four on the island by 1890. Questions soon arose among the islanders and the British government as to whether a population of this size could survive.

In 1904 the government made a proposal that all islanders would be transferred to Cape Colony provided all agreed. So it was put to the vote. Ten out of the sixteen families voted to stay on the island and the proposal was scrapped.

The future of Edinburgh, Tristan, looked bleak once again in August 1961 when a wide fissure developed on the volcanic island. Rock crumbled from the side of the mountain and earth tremors were felt. At first everyone was evacuated to the potato patches on the island but as it became clear that the volcano was now active the islanders were moved twenty five miles to Nightingale Island, and later to Cape Town. As the islanders passed Tristan on their way to Cape Town they could see the smoke and lava gushing from their island.

The islanders were later transferred to Southampton, England where they were given accommodation. They remained in Britain for two years after which the island was reported to be safe and the majority of the Tristan Da Cunha residents returned to their homes.

The short stay in England was upsetting but it did have its benefits. Today there is running water and electricity for the islanders and many of the thatched roofs have been replaced by corrugated sheeting. In 1971 a hospital was built and four years later a school was introduced which serves the eighty families who now live in Edinburgh, Tristan Da Cunha which remains the island's only village.

Fishing vessels from Cape Town, South Africa call at Tristan six times a year with accommodation for a few passengers and any urgent medical cases, providing Tristan's main external link. The only other regular passenger ship is the RMS *St Helena* which calls at the island once a year as it passes en route from England to Cape Town.

Edinburg, Texas USA was once named Edinburgh, but for no apparent reason on February 14th, 1911, by resolution of the commissioner's court the 'h' was dropped from the town's name. This was the Texan town's second name change. The first was more dramatic than the second. The town was called Chapin, originally after Dennis B Chapin. But he was accused of homicide in 1911 and although he was acquitted the residents believed that Chapin was no longer a suitable name for the town and adopted Edinburgh as the new title.

The name of Edinburg was chosen to honour the birthplace of John McAllen, an early Scots pioneer who had ventured through the area along the Rio Grande before the middle of the nineteenth century. Edinburg, Texas is now the largest citrus and vegetable shipper in the State, and nearby oil and gas fields boost the economy of the town which has around 30,000 inhabitants.

Edinburg is also the spelling used in nine other towns around the world named after Scotland's capital city. In most situations it is not clear why residents decided to drop the 'h' at the end.

Another example of this is Edinburg, New York which was first settled in 1787 by Abijah Stark and his family. They were soon followed by a group of settlers attracted by cheap land and more 'elbow room'. Many of them had already seen the area as they had served in the War of Independence.

By 1801 there were enough settlers to declare a township and it was given the name of Northfield on March 13th, 1801. It wasn't until 1808 that it was discovered there was a town of the same name in New York State and a meeting was held to decide on a new name. The residents met in the house of Squire James Goodwin, and there are two stories describing what happened at that meeting. One story claims that Mrs Goodwin agreed to brew a mug of steaming 'flip' for everyone at the meeting if she could choose the name of the town. Others say that George Bradford, a Scotsman living nearby asked for the town to be named after the capital city in his native land.

Nobody knows whether or not the residents got their mug of 'flip', a sweet drink made from wine or cider, but it is certain that during the meeting the name was changed to Edinburgh.

In the 1905 census the town's name was spelt Edinburgh, but by 1915 it was shortened to Edinburg. Why? Again nobody knows.

The early industries of Edinburg, New York included farming, logging and woodenware manufacturing prospered until the1880s when a number of fires destroyed many of the town's mills. As a result the town almost disappeared as around a third of the residents moved elsewhere to find jobs. Disaster struck the area again in the 1920s as talk was underway that a dam was going to be built and the valley flooded. People living in the valley moved fearing that they could lose their homes if they stayed.

Edinburg, North Dakota however, did disappear when it was destroyed by fire in 1900. The fire destroyed the entire business area of the village having started at the rear of the drug store. Two people died in the flames and the economic loss was tremendous. But even before the ruins had stopped smoking the villagers had met to discuss the future and within a year the entire village was rebuilt. This was the second occasion when the residents had shown their determination to ensure the survival of their community.

It too was first known as Edinburgh, named after the Scots capital by a Norwegian, Christian Buck! Buck chose the name of Edinburgh to honour the university in Scotland where he received his education. Buck became the first postmaster of Edinburgh when a post office was established on November 1st 1882. Until then the post was mailed from Dundee, some six miles east.

In 1884 meetings were held in the neighbouring town of Garfield to promote the construction of a railroad to serve Edinburgh and the surrounding towns, but the route of the railroad was changed to by-pass both Edinburgh and Garfield. Garfield was abandoned as people left to other towns, but the residents of Edinburgh were not happy to move to a different town – so they moved their town, buildings and all, to a new location on the railway route! For some reason during its relocation Edinburgh became Edinburg. The new site was incorporated as Edinburg, which it remains to the present day.

A plaque was erected in 1975 to mark the spot of Old Edinburgh, North Dakota, which was established in 1882, but moved to the new site just five years after, in 1887. The plaque was laid as a bicentennial project sponsored by the Edinburg Civic League.

The residents of Edinboro, Pennsylvania had good reason to alter the spelling of their town when it was named after Edinburgh, Scotland. It is believed that the 'burgh' was changed to 'boro' as it was easier to pronounce for the settlers who were not familiar with the Scottish city.

A brochure on the town points out that in Scotland, 'burgh' is pronounced 'boro', so that in the United States 'Edinburgh' was changed to 'Edinboro'. The residents of Scotland's capital city may dispute this pronunciation of their city's name.

General George Washington travelled through where Edinboro stands today in 1753, bound for Fort Boeuf and entered an account of the area into his daily journal. A Scot, William Culbertson read the general's glowing description forty years later and surveyed the site for the Holland Land Company. The following year William

Culbertson led the first settlers to the area destined to be called Edinboro. Culbertson led a group of settlers over the Appalachian Mountains by horse-drawn wagons and oxen and when they arrived they immediately cleared the land and built their town.

William Culbertson first named the site Washington but one of the group, a Mrs Campbell, pointed out to him that there was already a Washington in Pennsylvania. William Culbertson's wife insisted that the settlement was named after Edinburgh, Scotland, the home of their ancestors.

Edinboro was incorporated in 1840 and today has a population of 7,700. The main 'industry' of Edinboro is the university which has 8,000 students, meaning that the students outnumber townsfolk.

The Edinboro University of Pennsylvania has kept the Scottish tradition of the town alive by naming the streets on the campus after places in Scotland. Students even named their football and baseball teams 'The Fighting Scots' and the female sports teams are called 'The Lady Scots'. In honour of the town's Scottish roots the university holds a Scottish Festival, organised by the Robert Burns Society and a bagpipe school is run for the pipers.

Not all the towns named after Edinburgh, Scotland are so Scots conscious. The residents of Edinburg, Illinois for example, have lost touch with their Scottish roots. Although the town has been named after Edinburgh, Scotland it is not known how it got its name. The village and surrounding area was surveyed by Abraham Lincoln, who later became President of the United States. And as the village became a popular stagecoach stop, the hotel was used by Lincoln as he went on his travels as a young state politician.

When the town was incorporated the Scottish spelling of Edinburgh was used until 1894 at which time the spelling was altered to Edinburg. The town was established in 1873 beside the town of Blueville. There was great rivalry between the two settlements but this was resolved on August 8th, 1874 when a merger was approved in a vote. Despite Blueville being the older of the two, the Edinburg residents obviously got their way in naming the merged settlement. The population of Edinburg, Illinois now stands at little under 1,000 and is mainly a farming community.

There are several other towns named after the Scottish capital. Edina, Minnesota USA, derives its name from the Scottish city,

61

developing around a flour mill, itself named Edinburgh.

Edina, Missouri was named by a Scottish emigrant.

Edinburgh, Virginia, USA was named after the Scottish capital.

There are also Edinburgs in Indiana, Mississippi, Missouri, New Jersey, Maine and Virginia in the United States.

In addition there is a district called New Edinburgh in Ottawa, Canada. And a New Edinburg in Arkansas.

There are also settlements called Leith in Ontario in Canada, and in Alabama, Arkansas, North Dakota and Nevada in the USA.

Despite its name Edinburg, Latvia has not been named after Edinburgh, Scotland. The resort in the city of Rigas was named after the 'Garden of Eden'. As was the town of Edenburg in South Africa's Orange Free State.

Fife

F ife, Scotland is often described as 'the Kingdom' because
of its self-contained nature, being bounded by water on three
sides by the Firths of Tay and Forth and the North Sea. Although
the county measures only 21 mileswide and 46 miles long at the
widest points, the coastline measures 115 miles.

The area was important in pre-industrial Scotland containing
three of Scotland's most important towns of that period –
Dunfermline, Falkland and St Andrews. The latter of course, is the
world famous 'home' of golf which has a number of namesakes
spread across the globe.

No fewer than twelve places share the St Andrews which is home
to the famous Royal and Ancient Golf Club founded in 1754. Few
realise that the Scottish golfing resort was not always called St
Andrews. It first carried the title Muckross which means 'boar-wood'
in Gaelic. This was later changed to Kilrymont, meaning 'Church on
the royal mount' and, later again, to Kilrule, 'Church of St Regulus'.
The final change happened when the place was renamed to honour
the Church of St Andrew in 1144.

St Andrews is not only the home of golf but is home to Scotland's
oldest university which was established in the fiteenth century. The
Fife burgh now has a population of 11,136.

Not all of the towns called St Andrews have been named after
the Scottish burgh, but St Andrews New Brunswick, shares more
than its name with the Scottish town as it too is a golfing and fishing
resort. St Andrews is one Canada's oldest towns being founded in
1783 by United Empire loyalists from Maine. Streets are named after
King George III, the Queen, the Princess Royal and the Prince of
Wales confirming the town's loyalist origin. The local church was
named Greenock Church after the Scottish town by local resident,

Christopher Scott. The front of the church bears an emblem of a 'green oak' which is said to symbolise the name of the church.

Among the places named after the Fife town which bears the name of Scotland's patron saint, is Saint Andrew, Guernsey, Jamaica and Trinidad.

There is a Saint Andrew, Auckland in England which is also known as South Church and a Saint Andrews Major which is a village in Glamorgan, Wales.

Saint Andrew Bay in Florida is an arm of the Gulf of Mexico in Bay County while Saint Andrew Channel is an arm of the Bras d'Or in Cape Breton Island, Nova Scotia with an opening to the Atlantic. Saint Andrews East is a village in Quebec on the North River near its mouth on the Ottawa River.

There are two Saint Andrews Islands, one of which is in the Gambia, the other in the Caribbean Sea off the coast of Nicaragua, belonging to Colombia. And St Andrews, South Carolina is a large unincorporated district with 25,000 residents, which is largely a residential suburb of Columbia.

Whilst St Andrews is one of Canada's oldest towns, Newburgh is one of the oldest towns in New York State. The history of the town began on September15, 1609 when Henry Hudson sailed into Newburgh Bay. It was around a century after Hudson's visit that the first house was built in Newburgh which is believed to be the oldest in the county. It is also believed to be the oldest house in America built by a member of the Jewish religion. It was constructed by Lewis Moses Gomez, a Spanish nobleman who established a fur trading post with the Indians. This was the first development of trade between Europeans and the native Indians. Gomez went on to become one of the wealthiest merchants in New York before his death in 1722.

Although the New York town may be named in its own right as the name refers to 'New Borough' it is more likely that it has been named after the town of the same name in Fife as the Newburgh title was first used during an influx of Scots settlers.

Newburgh, New York has been dubbed the 'Crossroads of the Northeast' by truckers who travel the Route 87 and Route 84 which intersect here. The town is becoming a business centre in the northeast of New York and its population has grown to around 25,000.

The Scottish version of Newburgh is a small royal burgh in Fife, founded in 1191, which owes its existence to Lindores Abbey which stands on the Firth of Tay facing Mugdrum Island. Weaving and later linoleum were the largest employers until the late nineteenth century, since when Newburgh, Fife has remained a one street town.

Another town to be named after a Fife community is Kincardine, Ontario whose flag displays the Scottish flag with a maple leaf while the town crest on the right contains the thistle, the emblem of Scotland. Other Scottish influences in the Canadian town can be seen by the street names which include MacDonald Avenue, McGraw Drive, Dunsmoor Park and Elgin House.

However the first visitors to the Kincardine area of Canada were not Scottish but Jesuit missionaries and French explorers who came during the early part of the seventeenth century. They encountered the Tobacco and/or Wyandotte Indian tribes who hunted and fished in the area. The Indian treaty which surrendered this part of the country was not signed until August 1836 when the Indians were offered "twelve hundred and fifty pounds per annum, as long as grass grows and water runs".

Shortly after the treaty was concluded by Sir Francis Bond Head immigrants began arriving in Upper Canada. In 1845 there were 25,375 immigrants, but by 1847 this had increased to 89,440. This helped double the population of Upper Canada from 486,055 in 1842 to almost one million by 1852.

In 1848 Captain A Murray MacGregor put into the mouth of the Penetangore river and dropped off Allan Cameron and William Withers with a few provisions. These men were Kincardine's first settlers. Today Kincardine, Ontario has a population of around 60,000 and industries include knitting and woollen mils, a furniture factory and salt work. However the largest employer is the nearby Bruce Nuclear Power Development – its namesake in Scotland is flanked by the Longannet and Kincardine power stations.

There are a number of other Kincardines in Scotland such as Kincardineshire county in the north east, Kincardine in Ross and Cromarty, and Kincardine O'Neil which is located south of Aberdeen. But the Canadian version took its name from the town on the Firth of Forth.

The name Kincardine comes from the Gaelic word 'cinn'

meaning 'at the head of' and the Brittonic word 'carden' meaning wood.

There are several other places on the world map bearing Fife placenames. Not all of them however were named after their Scottish counterpart.

Lochgelly, West Virginia for example was not named after the town in Fife, Scotland but after a coal company from the Scots town. The West Virginian community was first called Stuart when it was named by coal operator Samuel Dixon in honour of the Royal house in Scotland. However the name was changed in 1907 after a mining accident killed eighty four men following an explosion.

Dixon, who had experienced difficulties in hiring new miners after the disaster, believed that a name change would rid the settlement of it morbid past. He decided to name the mining town after the Lochgelly Coal and Iron Company which was owned by an associate of his in Scotland.

There are several other examples.

Despite their name, the Falkland Islands in the South Atlantic were not named after the famous Scottish town in Fife. They were named after Anthony Cary, the 5th Viscount Falkland by Captain John Strong who made the first recorded landing in 1690.

Leslie, Fife does not derive from a Christian or family name but comes from the Gaelic words 'lios' meaning 'garden' and 'linn' meaning 'pool', standing for 'the garden of the pool'.

It is possible however that some of the seven places throughout the United States and South Africa that bear the same name have been named after a person and not the Scottish version.

One such place is Leslie County in Kentucky, USA which was named after Governor Preston H Leslie who was governor of Kentucky from 1871-1875. The county covers an area of 1200 acres and is almost totally forested. The entire Leslie county is situated in the Redbird Unit of the Daniel Boone National Forest.

Leslie, Scotland was a flax and bleaching burgh which is home to Leslie House, the former seat of the Earls of Rothes. The house was partially destroyed by fire on Christmas Day 1763. The surviving section was rebuilt and used as a private house until the 1950s since when it has been a Church of Scotland eventide home.

There are several other places named Leslie including towns in

Idaho, Arkansas, Georgia, Michegan and Missouri. How they got their names, as with so many of the placenames mentioned in this book, is still the subject of speculation. Readers may have been able to find out some answers.

There is also a community called Leslie in the Transvaal, South Africa which lies close to a town called Leven, both of which were named by two Patterson brothers. Leven is named after the town at the mouth of the River Leven in Fife. The Patterson brothers were responsible for surveying the railway line between Spring and Bethel in the early 1900s and were also responsible for naming Kinross. The two brothers are believed to have come from Scotland.

There is a village called Fife Lake in Manitoba and a village of Fife in Texas. The Texas community did not have a name until 1902 when a post office was established in the local store. The name was suggested by Mrs Agnes Blythe Finlay, wife of James Finlay, one of the town's founders, after her home county in Scotland.

The Finlays arrived at the same time as another family from Scotland, the Mitchells. The Mitchells bought up land and established the Mitchell Land and Cattle Company in 1909 selling tracts of land where Fife now stands. According to a local history book on the Fife area, many of the Scottish traditions were kept alive in the town including the tendency for daughters and sons to benamed after paternal and maternal grandparents. "This accounts for the many Roberts and Margarets around Fife," explains the book.

Cupar is a village in south Saskatchewan, forty miles NNE of Regina.

Cupar in Fife, Scotland is the county town of Fife and in ancient times the home of the MacDuff Earls of Fife. Nothing remains of their castle today, even though Castlehill is a permanent reminder of the town's proud past. Cupar was granted a burgh charter in the fourteenth century.

The town's name derives from the Gaelic 'comhpairt' which means 'common pasture'.

Glasgow

The official letterhead of
the town of New Glasgow,
Nova Scotia bears thistles
and a lion rampant, with
the inscription, "Let New
Glasgow Flourish"

G lasgow, once the second city of the British Empire, exported
more than goods to every corner of the globe – it exported
its name.

During the eighteenth century, Glasgow, Scotland became the
major port in trade with America by exporting goods which were in
demand amongst colonies in exchange for imports. Exports included
hard-wearing cloths, iron implements for farming, carpentry and
building, glass and leather goods which were exchanged for rum
and tobacco.

The name Glasgow became a popular export too. Nine Glasgows
in the United States, one in Canada and two in Jamaica are a
permanent reminder of the Scottish city's former role.

It was the introduction of the company store system that made
Glasgow's Tobacco Lords so successful in the importation of tobacco
to Britain. This was a simple system under which the Glasgow

tobacco firms established stores in the colonies run by employees of the firms. They both collected the tobacco and provided the growers with consumer goods which were brought over from Scotland. The goods were often sold on credit to the tobacco planters on condition that they sold their tobacco to the company. Advances were often repaid in tobacco and merchants kept the price of the tobacco low so that it took a long time for the planters to settle the credit.

The company store system had obvious advantages over the system used by merchants in England who sold the tobacco on behalf of the planters on a commission basis, but it did have its risks.

The downfall for this lucrative trade came with the onset of the American War of Independence which made it impossible for the Glasgow merchants to collect their debts from the planters. The merchants estimated that planters owed them in excess of £1,300,000, only part of which was paid back in 1811 following legal action.

The War of Independence, which began in 1775 also hampered the supply of tobacco to Scotland. Glasgow's Tobacco Lords, who in 1771 imported a staggering 47,000,000lb of tobacco, most of which was re-exported, mainly to France, received less than 300,000lb in 1777, two years after fighting broke out. Although trade picked up the following year in, 1778 the total trade of Scotland was still little more than half of that imported in 1771.

Another large factor in emigration from Glasgow was the rising population during the eighteenth century. In 1708 there were 12,500 people living in the city but by 1750 this figure had doubled.

Much of the Potomac region of Virginia was settled due to the 'Glasgow store system' such as the town of Dumfries which lies on the Potomac River and became a major shipping point for tobacco to Scotland. Nearly all storekeepers in this area of Virginia at the time were said to be Scots.

At one time there was a town in Virginia called New Glasgow although its name was later changed to Clifford. Glasgow, Kentucky, USA is one of the Glasgows in the United States to have tobacco amongst its early industries. It was formed in 1799 as the county seat of Barren County, Kentucky on 152 acres of land owned by John Gorin, who is remembered as the first resident of the town. Tobacco is still among the industries of Glasgow, Kentucky.

The location of the town had been a subject of controversy. Whilst John Gorin wished it to be laid out at the site of his Big Spring, his competitor, Richard Garnett wanted the county seat to be at the site of his spring a few miles northwest. To determine the location of the new town an election was held and the winner, by just a few votes was John Gorin's Big Spring site, through which water still flows.

There has been some confusion around how the town came to be called Glasgow. John Gorin's son, Franklin Gorin, said in his recollections of the town which were published in the *Glasgow Times* in 1876 that the town was named after Glasgow, Virginia. Others disputed this, saying that the town had been named after Glasgow Scotland, a name chosen by one of the many Scottish settlers in the area.

This is more likely as, although there was a town in Virginia called New Glasgow at the time, one of Glasgow, Kentucky's first trustees, John Matthews is said to have come from Glasgow, Scotland.

Governed by five trustees, the town laid down local by-laws in 1809. Any person found guilty of shooting or racing horses in the town would be fined two dollars, or if a slave, be whipped.

Not all towns outlawed horse racing however. In an early photo of Glasgow, Montana there can be seen a horse race down the Main Street. Up until the late nineteenth century the land on which Glasgow, Montana now stands lay in a large Indian reservation, but in 1887 the St Paul, Minneapolis & Manitoba Railroad Company purchased a right of way through the land. White settlement was only allowed inside the right of way which measured 150 feet wide though increasing to 500 feet at each stopping point.

From April 2nd until October 15th 1887 it took up to 9,000 builders and 7,000 horses to complete the 570 mile railtrack from Minot, North Dakota to the Great Falls. A man named Charles Hall, from Philadelphia learned that the railroad was to have a division at a wide point in the Milk River Valley, so named because the river is said to be colour of "a tablespoon of milk in a dish of tea". Hall arrived in the area to 'welcome' the rail. He reached the area with his Indian lady companion and his horse, Sookey, which pulled his belongings on an Indian travois. He built a log cabin which became his house and headquarters, the first house in Glasgow.

Hall later claimed the township and became Glasgow's first postmaster but, it was not Charles E Hall who got to name the town Glasgow. Nor was it one of the Scots settlers to arrive in Glasgow in the following years. In fact it was not even a resident of the town who chose its name.

In October 1887 the siding, the forty fifth west of Minot, was still known as 'siding 45' and with the railroad moving in, it was a railroad clerk in Minot who decided that this was not a proper name for the growing settlement. Stuck on what to call the place, the clerk took a world map in his hand and Glasgow, Scotland caught his eye. Seven years later, in 1894 the division four miles west of the new town known as Stockholm had its name changed to Paisley after the Paisley near Glasgow in Scotland.

In the winter of 1887 a treaty was made between the Indians and the government which allowed white settlement in the county and on May 9th 1888, a telegraph from Washington DC reached Glasgow to say that the country outside the right of way was now open for white settlement. That very night five saloon tents were set up to await the arrival of the thirsty settlers.

In the first year of its existence, Glasgow was visited by a writer from the Troy, New York, *Daily Times*, who described the site as a 'Mushroom Western City.'

He wrote, "Glasgow is one of many picturesque towns along the Manitoba railroad. It is a mushroom village and probably not more than a few months old. There is but one street, and that faces the railroad station. The houses happen to be tents, with two or three exceptions, and in front of each, over the door in large black letters more than a foot high, the word saloon indicated the nature of the refreshment that might be expected within."

By 1890 Glasgow had an estimated population of between five and six hundred largely due to the heavy advertising from the railroad who claimed in the *St Paul & Minneapolis Pioneer Press* on July 1st, 1889, "Glasgow is not a town to be; it is. To the home seeker it offers its wealth of free government lands, and all the facilities and comforts to be found in a well-established town."

Glasgow's mushroom growth almost backfired however when the *Valley County Gazette* in April 1894 claimed, "The lost Eldorado has been found!"

Gold fever hit Glasgow's residents and the article was headlined, "Eureka! Clerks, cowboys and strikers rushing to the goldfields, press every available team and horse into service. Town almost evacuated."

For thirty years miners in the area had searched in vain to find the lost Kies mine. In January Z W Alexander, one of the old miners in the country, discovered gravel containing from three to eighteen colours to the pan and thought he had found the legendary lode.

There were rumours that the mine was a 'rank fake', but even the most experienced of miners were convinced that it was 'the real thing'. And prospectors rushed to stake a claim on the field. An article in the *Gazette* said that the rumours had been started by "pernicious liars who were thwarted in getting a good claim for themselves."

A mining camp sprung up to cope with the influx of prospectors and was named Alexander City after the man who found the mine, but the tent town was not to survive long. Less than two months after its first newspaper article claiming that the lost Eldorado had been found, the *Gazette* read, "Our hopes vanished." The goldfields had not lived up to the prospectors' expectations and by early June, Alexander City was left abandoned and the disheartened claimants returned to Glasgow which had been in danger of becoming a ghost town. Although gold did exist in Alexander City and the fields did provide a wage for some prospectors, gold speculating was never one of Glasgow's main sources of wealth.

Glasgow's population exploded once again in 1913 when the Fort Peck Indian Reservation was opened for homesteading by white settlers. This had been widely advertised and the names of all interested parties were put into a container. The lucky ones whose names were drawn 'won' themselves a homestead.

One of the disappointed candidates whose name was not chosen was Harry S Truman who went on to become President of the United States. Had Truman won a homestead he might have followed in his father's footsteps who was a small farmer in Missouri and world history might have been quite different. Instead he entered politics and Truman, who was Vice-President when Roosevelt died in April 1945 moved into the White House. Within months he had authorised the dropping of atomic bombs on Japan.

Not all the Glasgows have flourished like this Montana city. Over two thousand kilometres east lies Glasgow, Pennsylvania. Situated on the Ohio River in Beaver County, the town once had a population of over 3,000 but numbers have dwindled in recent years to around 70. The town was laid out in October 1836 by Sandford C Hill, surveyor, on a tract of land owned by George Dawson.

The population of Glasgow initially soared in 1860 when new techniques in oil production were introduced. For years the Seneca Indians had collected oil as it oozed from the ground but with the invention of the oil rig there began a race for the oil. Prospectors from all over came in hope to find more of the 'black gold' and at one time their was said to be an oil rig in just about every yard in the Borough of Glasgow, Pennsylvania. An oil refinery was built in Glasgow but the oil did not last and the refinery was destroyed by fire in 1920.

By 1946 the population of the borough of Glasgow had fallen to just 300, and by the 1980 census this had fallen to 106. The latest census in 1990 shows there are only seventy people living in Glasgow. The residents are happy at this though and Dan Gallagher, mayor of Glasgow, the smallest municipality in Beaver county said, "It's quiet here. Tranquil." There are no industries based in Glasgow and there are no shops, but Glasgow's residents don't believe that the tiny town is ever going to fade out of existence.

Not much larger than the Pennsylvanian borough is the district of Glasgow in the parish of Saint Elizabeth, Jamaica. The future of the small farming community east of White Hill has looked bleak as more citizens migrate from the district in order to make a better life for their families.

Glasgow district is so remote that it took several months for the Saint Elizabeth Parish Council to locate Glasgow for my research. A parish council official described the village, "The roads are in disrepair with trees overhanging and heavy growth of shrubs which form a lush vegetation." There is no electricity supply and their water supply is obtained from household tanks. The population of the district is approximately two hundred with residents engaged in farming. Crops cultivated include pimento, cocoa, coffee, banana and yam.

The town of New Glasgow, Nova Scotia was named after

Glasgow, Scotland by one of the early settlers, William Fraser who on arrival at the settlement in 1785 proclaimed that he saw "another Clyde and another Glasgow." Fraser got his way as far as naming the settlement but the river was actually named the East River.

The first handful of settlers arrived in Pictou County in which New Glasgow lies in 1767. They came from Maryland and Pennsylvania and were joined six years later by 189 Scots who sailed from Scotland on the *Hector*.

These early Scots settlers named several early settlements after their homeland and today the area has an abundance of Scottish placenames such as Glengarry, Lorne, Elgin and Gairloch. Other Scots followed and in 1819 a group of distressed weavers from Scotland arrived in Glasgow, Pictou County, probably attracted by the familiar name of the settlement.

The discovery of coal near the site of New Glasgow in 1798 gave a boost to the area and brought about the development of iron and steel industries very similar to Glasgow, Scotland. New Glasgow like its namesake is today surrounded by coal mines, many of which are now disused. Another similarity between the two cities is that New Glasgow, Nova Scotia was for a time a thriving shipbuilding centre.

New Glasgow has kept its Scottish heritage alive in the form of two annual events – the popular Festival of the Tartans and a Highland games. The town has also kept in touch with its Scottish counterpart and a few years ago the then Lord Provost of Glasgow, Scotland, Susan Baird visited New Glasgow. In 1993 Lord Provost Bob Innes also made a visit during the Festival of the Tartans.

Not all of the international Glasgows have been named after Scotland's largest city. One in particular in Missouri was named after a man called James Glasgow.

James Glasgow was one of the town's founders when it was incorporated in 1836. Settlement was first attempted in the Glasgow area in Missouri several years earlier at a time when the Missouri River banks were overgrown and the only way to reach the area was by boat – a dangerous trip with frequent attacks by hostile Indians.

In 1816 a town sprung up named Franklin to cope with the influx of settlers. This was a forerunner of Glasgow. In the 1820s shortly after the town was founded however, severe flooding wrecked the homes of the town's 1,000 residents. Franklin was replaced by Chariton in 1826 but this too was destroyed by flooding to be replaced by Monticello, later changed to Louisville-on-the-Missouri. However this may have proved too much of a mouthful for the residents and the community died.

Finally in 1836 Glasgow was established using the capital of a number of investors, including that of James Glasgow. In the beginning the Indians resisted the settlers, tensions mounted, hostilities broke out and by 1820 all of the native Americans had been either killed or forced away.

In the beginning tobacco and flour were Glasgow's main industries and the river soon established itself as the principal shipping point of goods. In 1849 Glasgow was declared a city whose exports included 4,000 hogsheads of raw tobacco, 5,000 boxes of processed tobacco and 2,500 bales of hemp. By 1852 there were thirteen tobacco manufacturers and stemmeries in the city and a staggering six and a half million pounds of tobacco was shipped from Glasgow's wharf, some of which was bound for Glasgow, Scotland.

The rich tobacco merchants in the Missouri city often had slaves who could be purchased for anything between $250 and $1,200. But in the 1860 election Abraham Lincoln, the Republican candidate who promised to wipe out slavery, swept the northern states winning the Presidency of the United States. By the time Lincoln was inaugurated as President the following year seven states had seceded from the union and one month after this on 14th April 1861 the American Civil War began when Confederate forces attacked Fort Sumpter, in Charlestown, South Carolina.

For a time the Confederates had a training and recruitment area in Glasgow, Missouri which caused the Union forces to send their army to ruin the recruitment efforts and occupy the town. At 5am on October 15th, 1864 Confederate General Price, sent two brigadier generals to the occupied town to attack after hearing that 5,000 small arms were being stored in the City Halls.

The Battle of Glasgow had begun and Glasgow was surrounded by Confederate troops, estimated to outnumber the Union troops by seven to one. However they did not give up without a fight. They were fighting a losing battle and after hours of fighting they surrendered after being assured that the 800 prisoners would be treated fairly.

Glasgow's troubles were not over as two days later a band of villains raided the city. It was not uncommon for General Price to enlist bandits as the Confederates were always in need of money.

Quantrill was one of these rogues for whom war allowed crimes of murder and thievery to be legalised. On the evening of October 17th Quatrill forced W F Dunnica, a partner of the bank, to open the bank vault. He left with $21,000. Luckily Dunnica had buried $32,000 the day before fearing that this may happen. Glasgow's other bank, the Glasgow Savings Bank was equally prepared and had taken all of their money to St Louis.

Quantrill never returned to Glasgow as he was shot a few months later on his way to Washington where he planned to assassinate President Lincoln. However a disciple of Quantrill arrived two or three weeks later to the home of Benjamin Lewis, one of the founders of Glasgow, and owner of one of the town's leading tobacco firms. Lewis had put a $6,000 reward for Bill Anderson 'Dead or Alive', but little did he expect 'Bloody Bill Anderson' to come to collect the bounty in person. Lewis was forced to give all his money to Anderson, which totalled $1,000. But this was not enough and he was held to ransom in the town until the residents came up with the other $5,000.

On April 9, 1865 General Lee surrendered to Ulysses Grant at Appomatox and the war ended. Later that year the eighteenth amendment to the United States Constitution was passed stating that, "Neither slavery nor involuntary servitude, except as a punishment for crime whereof the party shall have been duly convicted, shall exist within the United States, or any place subject to their jurisdiction."

However for several years Negro slavery remained as in Glasgow where former slaves continued to work for the white plantation owners.

The mid nineteenth century brought change to the river town with the introduction of railroads, but Glasgow was quick to react and fought hard for the Iron Horse. And in 1878 Glasgow was the proud location of the world's first all steel bridge, whose 800 tons of steel spanned the river.

Today the City of Glasgow has a population of around 1,300, and the largest employers are Standard Havens, a manufacturer of hot asphalt production equipment and American Recreation Products, who produce sleeping bags.

Today much has changed in the City of Glasgow, Scotland and although in recent years there have been a number of improvements to the city the population has fallen from over one million in 1951 to around 680,000 today.

Traditional industries such as shipbuilding, coal and steel have all but disappeared although there are still two active shipyards, Kvaerner at Govan and Yarrows. Much of the fall in population was due to a deliberate policy called overspill in which families were given homes in New Towns such as East Kilbride and Cumbernauld. These were built on greenfield sites as city slum dwellings were demolished.

Memories of the Scottish city's proud past can be seen in the Merchant City area of the town centre which is rapidly becoming a tourist attraction and in recent years Glasgow, Scotland has hosted the UK's Garden Festival and in 1990 was the European City of Culture.

Thousands of North American tourists now arrive at Glasgow International Airport on direct flights from Boston, New York and Toronto as descendants of emigrants who left the city return to visit relatives and trace their roots.

the Grampian Mountains from Dunkeld township, Victoria
Courtesy Dunkeld & District Historical Museum, Australia

Highlands

Today the Scottish Highlands is a popular tourist venue drawing people from all over the UK, Europe, the Far East, United States and Canada. Tourists take part in climbing, hillwalking, fishing and during the winter, skiing.

Such is the beauty and tranquility of the Highlands that few realise that as recently as two hundred years ago this spectacularly scenic region of mountains and glens was fairly well populated.

The reasons for emigration from the Highlands of Scotland are closely interlinked with the history of the country. And the most renowned reason for emigration was the Highland Clearances which led to thousands of Scots being driven from their homes.

The Clearances are said to have began around the early 1730s when the estates began the elimination of the clan system of land tenure. The tacksmen were responsible for collection of rents and some of them emigrated taking their tenants with them, mainly to North Carolina but also to Georgia, Pennsylvania, Ohio and Kentucky.

After the 1745 rebellion led by Charles Edward Stuart (Bonnie Prince Charlie) came the anti-Jacobite measures. The final ignominy of the conclusive defeat at Culloden moor in 1746 led to a whole raft of measures being introduced by the Hanovarian government in London to break up the clan system. As well the proscribing of the Gaelic tongue and even the playing of bagpipes, these included an acceleration in the dismantling of the system of land tenure.

In 1760 large tracts of Highland land was purchased, mainly by lowland farmers for sheep. This led to the clearance of thousands of tenants from their homes, first in Southern Argyll and Dunbartonshire then Inverness-shire, Ross and Sutherland. This continued and indeed increased in the first half of the nineteenth century, thus setting a pattern of migration that has prevailed to this day.

The majority of the Scots Highlanders were bound for USA and Canada. A few went to the other colonies and emigration to Australia became significant in 1852 when the Highland and Island Emigration Society was formed.

This has led to a concentration of towns named after the Highlands of Scotland in USA and Canada and there is a county named after Argyll in New South Wales, a Braemar in South Australia and a Lismore in New South Wales. However there are also communities called Huntly and Oban in New Zealand as well as an Oban in Nigeria.

One of the most documented Highland towns in Canada is the town of Kildonan, an area in the City of Winnipeg, Manitoba. It was named after Kildonan in Scotland which is said to have taken its title from a Pictish saint. Saint Donan was martyred on the Isle of Eigg in 617. But while Winnipeg, Manitoba now has a population in excess of 610,000 all that is left of Kildonan, Scotland is ruined homes.

The Countess of Sutherland is said to have been responsible for the clearance of the estate – indicated in her letters that exist today – threatening to replace any man refusing to join her regiment with sheep. Those who refused were evicted at once, but even those who had shown loyalty were later given the same treatment.

Canada's Kildonan was founded in 1812 by a group of Scottish crofters from Mull, Lewis and Argyll. Thomas Douglas, 5th Earl of Selkirk was amongst the first of these who settled on the banks of the Red River. Between 1812 and 1815 several shiploads of migrants sailed to Canada and made the journey west to Selkirk's colony. Many of them came from Sutherland but also from Orkney and Ireland. The Scottish parish that once had a population of 1,574 in 1811 had dwindled to 257 over the next twenty years.

Although Douglas was a lowlander he sympathised with the Highlanders as he foresaw more clearances and so organised several migrations from the Scottish Highlands, the first being in 1803 when he led a party of 800 to a settlement on Prince Edward Island. He later purchased 116,000 square miles of prairie land from the Hudson's Bay company where he established his Red River colony.

Around 700 people from Kildonan, Scotland applied for grants of land in Selkirk's settlement on the Red River. However Selkirk was allowed no more than 100. This suggests that all of those exiled were willing to go.

There had been a fur trading post here since 1738 but Lord Selkirk introduced the first permanent settlers into the area. The party of 100 who sailed across the Atlantic from Stromness on *The Prince of Wales* chose to emigrate – unlike other Highlanders who were driven out.

In 1972 the unified City of Winnipeg was created by amalgamating North Kildonan, City of West Kildonan, Old Kildonan, City of West Kildonan and nine other municipalities, towns and cities.

Fort William, another Canadian town was named by a Scot called William McGillivray, principal director of the North West Company. McGillivray's trapping company was bitterly opposed to Lord Selkirk's Red River Colony and during 1815-16 drove out the colonists. There were several clashes between the settlers and members of the North West Company which resulted in the Massacre of Seven Oaks in the summer of 1816 when Lord Selkirk, a shareholder of the Hudson's Bay Company gathered a mass of disbanded soldiers and seized the fort. The following years saw the fort occupied by one of the two companies as they fought over the control of the lucrative fur trade.

Fighting ended in 1821 when the companies joined forces but as a result Fort William was eventually abandoned as the newly united company moved their headquarters to Hudson Bay.

However, contrary to what its name might suggest, Fort William in Ontario, Canada was not named after the small community near Scotland's Ben Nevis, nor the fort built by General Monk in the 1654 naming it Inverlochy. The fort held out to the Jacobites in the 1715 and 1745 risings but finally was demolished in the nineteenth century to make way for a railway station.

Lismore, New South Wales is one of the few Australian towns to be named after a Scottish Highland community, namely the Isle of Lismore in Argyll. The placename means 'big garden' derived from the Gaelic words 'lios' meaning garden and 'mor' which means big. The ten mile long Scottish island which lies in the southern end of Loch Linnhe has been commonly referred to as paradise.

Its name was said to have been given by St Molug in the sixth century, who as folklore has it, beat his rival St Columba to the land by cutting off one of his fingers and throwing it onto the shore.

The city of Lismore with its population of 42,000 spread throughout 1267 square kilometres includes a district called Dunoon but, despite the Scottish name, the New South Wales town is mainly a Greek and Italian community.

The first white settler in the Lismore region was William Wilson whose Scottish wife Jane named the site. They arrived in 1843 and applied to buy 163 acres of land on the Richmond River. The region's first industry was timber. Then in the mid 1800s the sugar industry was introduced to the area and by 1869 Lismore grown sugar was selling for £36 a ton.

With the Lismore area containing three World Heritage Rainforests, National Parks, Nature Reserves and State Forests it is a major eco-tourist centre. Nicknamed the Rainbow Region, Lismore is situated in the Richmond and Tweed Valley which forms the richest area of rainforest in New South Wales.

The nickname Rainbow originates from the frigate HMS *Rainbow*, as it was Captain James Rous who named the river after his close friend, Charles 5th Duke of Richmond. Captain Rous discovered the area of New South Wales in 1828, 158 years after explorer James Cook sailed by the river mouth without noticing it. Rous found the area had rich soils and also a sizable native population. However it was not for another fifteen years that the first white settler, William Wilson built his home here.

Whereas Lismore, New South Wales consists today of mainly a Greek and Italian community, the residents of Highland, Illinois are mostly Swiss and German. In fact the Illinois town is home to the Swiss National Anthem because it was at his home in the town that poet Heinrich Bosshard wrote *Sempacherlied*,the poem that formed the basis of the Swiss national song.

The town was founded in 1831 by Swiss pioneers from Sursee in Switzerland led by Dr Kasper Koepfli. However in 1836 a Scot, General Joseph Semple, managed to convince the Swiss pioneers that the town and the area strongly resembled that of northern Scotland and the town was named Highland.

Another Canadian town is the settlement of Melfort in Saskatchewan which was first settled in 1892 under the name of Stoney Creek. However, in 1902 the town was moved to its present location where it was surveyed by the Canadian Pacific Railway. It was at this time that Mrs Reginald Beatty, the first lady settler in the district, was asked to name the town. She chose Melfort after her family's home in Argyll, Scotland.

When the CPR built their railway line through the site it established Melfort as a main trade and cultural centre for the surrounding area. Melfort remains an agricultural centre with a trading area population of 60,000. The Melfort Museum displays a reproduction of a log farm house with various pieces of farming equipment used by the early settlers. And each year Melfort's residents take part in Old Time Threshing Day on the Russ Harold farm near Melfort where they participate in harvesting the way it was done in the pioneer days.

Due to north east Saskatchewan weather extremes other tourist attractions of the city include popular ski resorts during the winter and during the summer hiking and fishing. The normal mean daily temperature varies from 25^0C in July to -24.9^0C in January. However it is not unknown for the temperature to rise above 38^0 in the summer and fall to -50^0C in the winter.

In 1903 Melfort, which lies in the Carrot River Valley in north east Saskatchewan, was incorporated. However today the settlement is a city with a population of 6,500.

Banff in Alberta, Canada is a picturesque town set in the Canadian Rocky Mountains located in the spectacular Banff National Park which covers 2543 square miles. Although the Cree, Kootenay and Plains Blackfoot Indian tribes have long lived here, the first recorded European to enter the Banff area was George Simpson, Governor of the Hudson's Bay Company in 1841.

In 1871 the Canadian Government fulfilled their promise to unite British Columbia with the other four provinces and began construction on a national railway through the Rocky Mountains. In 1883 the railway passed through Banff and the following year Lord Strathcona, a CPR Director christened the area Banff after his birthplace in the Highlands of Scotland.

It wasn't long before the natural attraction of the area caught the Canadian Pacific Railway Company and in 1888 they built the area's first tourist accommodation, the Banff Springs Hotel. Since then millions of people have visited the town and it is estimated that Banff National Park welcomes around 3.5 million visitors a year.

Banff is the oldest of Canada's natural reserves being established in 1885. It was named after the Scottish town of Banff where the ruins of MacDuff's castle lies. It is not certain where the original name came from. It could derive from the Gaelic word 'banbh' which mean land unploughed for one year. There are other suggestions however pointing to the Gaelic word for Ireland, 'Banba'.

Elgin, Scotland also has Irish roots as the name derives from the Gaelic 'Eilgin' which means 'little Ireland'. There was for a time an area in Elgin called Little Ireland. And in turn at least another four towns were named after Elgin. However it is not possible to say whether they were named after the Scottish town of Elgin or one of the Earls of Elgin who took their title from it.

The town of Elgin in Illinois has a third possibility as to why it received its Scottish name when it was founded in 1835. According to local history in Illinois the town was named after a hymn tune. The traditional account is that the town was named by a Scotsman, James T Gifford, who took the name from his favourite hymn *The Song of Elgin*.

However Elgin County and the town of Elgin in Ontario and Elgin in New Brunswick are more than likely to have taken their name from James Bruce the 8th Earl of Elgin (1811-1863) who was also Governor General of Canada between 1847 and 1854.

Grampian, Pennsylvania was named in 1809 by Samuel Coleman after the Grampian Mountains in Scotland as not only did he come from there but the area reminded him of his homeland.

The town of Huntly in New Zealand was named by an early Scots settler after his home town in Scotland. However the Maori name for the town is quite different being Rahuipuketo meaning 'Sanctuary of the Songbirds'.

Highland, Pennsylvania is one of the many towns of this name in the United States. But only this town and one other in Illinois have been named after the Scottish region.

A settlement called Lochaber grew up around a lake of the same name in Nova Scotia which was named after its Scottish counterpart by settlers from the Highland district and loch in Scotland.

The founders of Dunmaglass, Nova Scotia were Scottish settlers from an estate of the same name in Inverness-shire near Foyers and named their settlement after it.

There are also several communities named after the town of Oban such as one in Saskatchewan, another in New Zealand and two in Nigeria. The New Zealand version is the capital of Stewart Island positioned in the north east. Until the 1940s the town was known as Half Moon Bay, but it is said that the name may have been changed by Sir William Stewart, who gave his name to the island and who possibly came from Oban, Scotland.

Among the many other towns named after villages and towns in the Scottish Highlands are Argyle, Illinois; Argyll, New South Wales; Braemar, South Australia; Brechin, Ontario; Dingwall, Nova Scotia; Glamis, Saskatchewan and Nairn, Ontario.

Calgary, Alberta skyline –
a long way from Calgary Bay, Isle of Mull
Courtesy Calgary Economic Development Authority, Canada

Western Isles

Numerous factors led to the population exodus from the Hebridean Islands off the west coast of Scotland to all parts of the globe. Various towns and areas are named after the Hebridean Islands in Canada, Australia and Peru! There is even a chain of islands in the Pacific Ocean named the New Hebrides by Scots explorer, James Cook, as the jagged rocks and crags reminded him of the Scottish Hebridean islands.

The reasons for the emigration from the Islands of Scotland range from famine and crop failure, clearance and the collapse of local industries and rising rents.

One controversial factor that has been put forward was over-population. In 1775 the population of Skye, the largest of the Inner Hebrides in Scotland, was estimated at 11,250. But by 1841 this had doubled. Various theories have been put forward for the population increase including peace breaking out among the clans, discovery of the smallpox vaccine and the introduction of the potato crop which had a higher yield per acre than any previous crop.

The first factor that increased the emigration rate from the Hebrides of Scotland was the failure of the potato in 1745-46. Potato crops failed again in 1836 and 1846. The collapse of the kelp industry in 1815 was also a factor. This industry involved the burning of seaweed for the manufacture of a salt alkali and one of the reasons for the Highland Clearances was to provide cheap labour for the industry.

The kelp industry flourished for a few years before and after the turn of the nineteenth century, employing a large portion of the population on the west coast of Scotland and throughout the islands. The long wars with France meant that import duty was heavy but when these wars ended in 1815 the import duty was reduced allowing cheap imports from abroad thus killing the Scottish kelp industry.

The collapse brought about widespread unemployment, while at the same time rents rose dramatically and many families had no means of earning a living.The next seventy years saw 7,000 people being forced from their homes in Mull and Iona alone.

The Highland and Island Emigration Society, which began in 1852 was particularly active around the islands of Mull and Skye, sending the majority of their emigrants to Canada and Australia. Evidence of this exodus remains to this day in the placenames of these countries.

Calgary, Alberta was named after Calgary Bay on the Isle of Mull by Colonel Macleod of the North West Mounted Police, as the area reminded him of Calgary Bay in Scotland. Calgary is a Gaelic word for 'bay farm'.

Calgary Bay in Scotland played a part in emigration. When the oppressive lairds began to evict farmers and crofters in the 1820s ships used to be anchored in the Calgary Bay so that the refugees could be boarded and shipped to North America.

The Alberta settlement was first established around 1875 shortly after the Canadian 'Mounties' had completed a march westwards to Alberta and built a fort at the confluence of the Bow and Elbow Rivers, one of a chain of forts established to curb the growing whisky trade.

At first the new post was called Fort Brisebois after the officer in charge, Inspector Ephrem Brisebois. However Brisebois was despised amongst his men and as he had not received permission from his superiors to name the fort, it was decided that a new name had to be found. The assistant commissioner of the Mounties, Colonel A G Irvine, consulted Colonel James Macleod, who came up with Calgary as a suitable name for the newly established fort and trading post.

Colonel Irvine, under the wrong impression that the name meant 'clear running water' in Scots, thought the name was appropriate and agreed the change to Fort Calgary. It was many years later that it was discovered that Irvine's explanation of Calgary's meaning was incorrect. Apparently Macleod had visited Calgary Bay on the Isle of Mull where his sister's relatives owned a small castle called Calgary House, which stands to this day.

In 1881 the Canadian Calgary consisted of two stores, the North West Mounted Police barracks and the commanding officer's house but the site was expanded in 1883 when the Canadian Pacific Railroad arrived at the fort bringing settlers. Calgary quickly became a ranching and agricultural centre. Calgary's population rose from 600 to 1,000 within a year. Just ten years later, by January, 1894 Calgary was elevated to city status with almost 4,000 residents.

The Canadian Government in 1896, desperate to attract settlers to western Canada offered free land grants of 160 acres. This attracted over one million people to the prairies of Saskatchewan and Alberta by the outbreak of the First World War, by which time Calgary's population had risen to 50,000.

It was during this period that coal, gas, oil and minerals began to be exploited in the areas around Alberta city. The city's fortunes changed for the better in 1947 as oil discoveries at nearby Leduc transformed Calgary into the administrative centre of oil exploration in Canada.

By the 1970s Calgary had become an international oil centre and the city, which ranks third as the major head office centre in Canada now boasts the headquarters of companies such as PetroCanada Inc, Shell Canada Inc, Nova, ATCO Ltd and Canadian Foremost. Eighty six per cent of Canada's oil and gas companies and sixty per cent of coal producers have their headquarters in Calgary, giving the city the title of 'Energy Capital of Canada'.

On the lighter side Calgary has also been described as the 'Hot Air Balloon Capital of Canada', which is just one of the attractions that makes the city a major tourist destination.

Calgary's proximity to the Rocky Mountains, which not only offer spectacular landscapes, but the opportunity to ski, hike, camp and river raft makes it a tourist mecca. The annual Calgary Exhibition and Stampede Week celebrates the city's western heritage and is a major draw. In 1988 the city, with a population of 700,000 plus, gained international recognition by hosting the Winter Olympic Games.

Another Canadian town to boast a Scottish name is Tobermory, Ontario named by a homesick Scot after his home town on the Isle of Mull in Scotland. Tobermory is the chief town on Mull which lies off the coast of Argyll. The town is also one of Scotland's smallest burghs. Tobermory, Ontario is also a popular tourist attraction, with visitors being attracted by its harbour and surrounding waters.

The homesick Scot referred to in the guide book *The Beautiful Bruce Peninsula* was one of a group of Scottish fishermen, who in the 1830s sailed here to fish on the Great Lakes. The fisherman spotted a resemblance between the Canadian harbour and his native town of Tobermory, Scotland, perhaps because the two towns lie on natural harbours.

The similarities do not end there. Both towns once had thriving fishing industries, but the decline of the herring fishing in the Hebrides in the nineteenth century, and a similar decline in fishing around the Bruce Peninsula in Canada around 1930, means that both towns now rely heavily on tourism.

Treasure hunters flock to Tobermory Bay in Scotland because of the shipwrecked *Florida*, a galleon from the Spanish Armada which sank in 1588 reputedly carrying £300,000 worth of gold bullion. Divers flock to Canada's Tobermory to explore the waters surrounding the town which has seen at least twenty five ships meet their fate during the last century alone.

Over 8,000 divers travel to Tobermory, Ontario each year to survey the shipwrecks while the less adventurous admire the relics retrieved in the museum. The divers off Tobermory, Scotland have been less fortunate however, as little has been recovered from the *Florida* as it lies buried under nine metres of silt in eighteen metres of water.

Both towns can truly be described as 'identical twins' because in 1982 Tobermory, Ontario was officially twinned with its namesake on the Isle of Mull, Scotland.

Tobermory, Ontario is situated in the township of St Edmunds located at the very tip of the Bruce Peninsula on the coast of Fathom Five National Park, between Lake Huron and Georgian Bay. The Bruce Peninsula region remained unsettled by whites until the nineteenth century when the Canadian Government, under increasing pressure to open up new areas for the emigrants to settle, entered into a treaty with local Indian tribes.

In 1827 a treaty between the Indians of western Canada and the provinces of Upper Canada (now Ontario) saw the Indians surrender much of their land including parts of the counties of Perth, Huron, Bruce and Grey. Nineteen years later the Treaty of the Manitouwaning was signed, with the local Indians surrendering the townships of southern Bruce County to the Government and the land north of an imaginary line still belonging to the Saugeen Indians.

However as the number of settlers arriving in the area increased the land that had already been surrendered by the Indians was filling up. At the same time some of the settlers noticed that the land north of the dividing line was more fertile. They crossed and began farming on the Indian land causing hostilities to break out in 1855. This led to a further treaty being signed leaving the Indians with little more than a few reserves.

Throughout the nineteenth century it was common to see Indian encampments at Tobermory, and up until the First World War they would fish around the cape, selling their catches to merchants or fish companies in the town.

The Indians were not the only ones to fish the waters of the Great Lakes as it was Scots fishermen who named the site in the 1830s. It wasn't until the 1870s however that the first land sales were held and the settlers moved in. As the town developed a number of sawmills and lumber camps were established. The timber trade began to decline by the early 1900s and fishing once again played the major role in the economic life of Tobermory. This only lasted until the 1930s since when the population has declined to around 900. But despite several other names being suggested including 'Collins Inlet' and 'Townplot of Bury', the settlement's Scottish title has survived.

Islay, Scotland may be only about fifty miles south of Tobermory, Scotland, but around 1500 miles separates Tobermory, Ontario from the tiny hamlet of Islay, Alberta which takes its name from the island of Islay in Argyll, Scotland.

Islay is the most southerly of the Inner Hebrides. The Scottish island lies fifteen miles off the coast and lies just twenty three miles from the coast of Northern Ireland. Islay has a number of archaeological sites including standing stones and stone circles, chambered cairns and forts. Many of the placenames on the island originate from the Viking conquest and the settling of Islay from the ninth to the twelfth centuries.

Until January 1st, 1907 the Islay, Alberta community was known as Island Lake, and there has been some speculation as to how the settlement got its Scottish name. The most accepted account is described by Mr A B Tolmie of Peterborough, Ontario who wrote,

"Back in the 1880s and 1890s there was a great exodus from Victoria County to take advantage of homestead opportunities in the American and Canadian west."

Mr Tolmie claimed that most of these early emigrants went to the Dakotas, particularly North Dakota, including the relatives of the writer's father. One of these migrant relatives was a man named Gilchrist. That was until he bumped into Sam Hughes, a man with influence and knowledge in the planning of railroads. Hughes told Gilchrist he was wrong to go to the Dakotas, but Gilchrist said he had no intention of heading to the 'inaccessible lands' of the Canadian west.

Sam Hughes made Gilchrist the offer that if he settled in the Canadian west on a location recommended by Hughes, he guaranteed there would be a station within three miles. Soon after settling there was a station built near Gilchrist's farm.

Once settled, Gilchrist met a Mr McKenzie, the superintendent of the railway line and suggested that the station be called Islay as so many of the Islay people from Victoria County were settled in the area. McKenzie replied that there was already a station on the line named Islay but he would arrange to have it changed so that the Islay people could have their station. So on 1st January, 1907 the community was incorporated as a village and the name of the post office was officially changed from Island Lake to Islay, in honour of the Islay emigrants who had settled there.

We are told that the early pioneers had some strange ways of amusing themselves. Each July they held an Islay Sports Day with foot races and tug-of-wars, but one of the more unusual events was 'catching the greasy pig'! The pig was greased all over with lard and turned loose for participants to catch, the winner taking home the greasy animal.

The early inhabitants of Islay, Alberta may have participated in unusual activities, but they were not alone. The residents of Colonsay, Saskatchewan still take part in an Annual Giant Bubble Bath to mark the end of the summer season. Saskatchewan's Colonsay was born due to the construction of the Canadian Pacific Railroad who designated the spot where the community now stands as a town site.

Colonsay was incorporated as a village on October 6, 1910 and the following year workmen began building the station which was intended to be "the largest and finest along the line". For a time Colonsay became an important railway junction with an engine shed for two locomotives. However this was destroyed when a cyclone struck the town in 1919.

It is not only the town itself that has been named after the small island in the Inner Hebrides in Scotland, but the streets take their name from the Hebrides too. Streets names including Islay, Bute, Jura, Oronsay, Skye, Kintyre and Staffa are a reminder of the Scots influence in the town's development.

Today the town has around 430 inhabitants, with the largest employer being the Central Canada Potash mining company while the population of the Scottish Colonsay is almost 100. This means that the islands residents are greatly outnumbered by the 7,000 sheep and 500 cattle scattered throughout the sixteen farms on the island. The Scottish island measures eight miles long and three miles wide lying northeast to south west, giving it the title 'Eilean Tarsuing' which is Gaelic for cross lying island. Colonsay has many archaeological and historic sites including standing stones, an Iron Age fort and the remains of a township deserted in the 1920s.

Also in Canada, the settlement of Dunvegan took its name from the town of Dunvegan and nearby Dunvegan castle on the Isle of Skye. Dunvegan castle claims to have been continuously occupied by the same family for longer than any other Scottish castle, being the seat of the MacLeod family since the thirteenth century.

The modern castle consists of a thirteenth century wall of enclosure, a fourteenth century keep, dungeon, kitchen and the Fairy Tower. The latest part of the castle, the Rory Mor house was built in the 1770s.

Tourists come to view the castle and its relics which include a Fairy flag, a talisman and the Rory Mor's Horn, an ancestral drinking cup from which it is claimed the heir to the chiefship has to drink a bottle and a half of claret in one go. The present chief, the 29th claims to have accomplished this feat in one minute and fifty nine seconds!

The community in Nova Scotia was at one time known as Broad Cove Marsh but this name was dropped in 1885 in favour of Dunvegan, no doubt chosen by a Scots emigrant.

Canada boasts another settlement called Dunvegan, this time on Cape Breton Island which attracted many settlers from the Highlands and Islands in the early nineteenth century. In the years 1826-27 alone, 2,000 people left Tobermory and Stornoway, Scotland, destined for Cape Breton Island.

Whilst Dunvegan in Skye is situated only around five miles from the Scottish village of Orbost, on the other side of the world map is another Orbost. The name of Orbost was given to the town in Victoria, Australia by its first settler, William McLeod after his home, a tiny village on the Isle of Skye.

However, McLeod's settlement, which is located 375 kilometres east of Melbourne has now outgrown the Hebridean village as Orbost Shire is the third largest shire in the state of Victoria. The Victoria shire extends 3,676 square miles and boasts a population of around 6,200. Its namesake in Scotland consists of a handful of houses.

The first settler in the Orbost district of Victoria was Peter Imlay, the son of a Scottish doctor who had brought 800 head of cattle from New South Wales. Imlay did not stay long however as the local aborigines became hostile and speared his cattle. He finally fled with only 500 cattle left.

It was at this stage the McLeod brothers bought Imlay's brand and established their station at Orbost. The McLeods named their new home after Orbost on the Isle of Skye, Scotland. The first land sales took place in 1881 and continued until 1885. By 1890 the settlement had begun to form. Two years later it was proclaimed as Croajingolong Shire, which must have been quite a mouthful as a year later the name was changed to Orbost. The primary industries of the shire are mainly agricultural, including seed-beans, maize growing, dairying, beef and cattle and timber mills.

Among other communities named after the Hebrides are Islay Province in Peru, a tiny village called Stornoway in southern Quebec and Tobermory in Queensland.

Orkney & Shetland

The Northern Isles of Orkney and Shetland were first colonised before 3,500 BC where the first inhabitants built the earliest surviving stone houses in Britain. There are also two henge monuments in the Orkneys, one of which, the 'Ring of Brogar', once consisted of sixty stones. Indeed Orkney has the largest concentration of prehistoric monuments that have been discovered in Europe.

There are two possible sources of the name Orkney. It has been suggested that the name refers to 'island of the Orc'. However the most accepted version is that the name derives from the Norse words 'orkn' meaning 'seal' and 'ey' meaning 'island'.

The Shetland Islands are the most northerly point of Great Britain where in midsummer, with the sun falling just 6^0 below the horizon there is constant daylight. The Shetland Islands were first called Inse Cat or Cat Islands after the tribe of 'Cats' which also occupied Caithness. Their name was changed after the Norse invasion to Hjaltisland from the personal name of Hjalti. They have also been referred to, although less common now, as the Zetland Islands as 'z' is the old Scots 'y' which is the phonetic spelling of the Norse 'hj'.

Amongst the places named after the Scottish islands are the South Orkney Islands and the South Shetland Islands in Antarctica which were both discovered and named by British sealers in the nineteenth century. The South Orkney Islands were discovered by George Powell, a British sealer and Nathaniel Palmer, an American. They were named because of their close proximity to the South Shetland Islands which were discovered two years previously.

However the South Shetland Islands, which were named in 1819 by William Smith would have been more accurately named after the Orkneys as these correspond better to their geographic relationship to the mainland. Shetland is also the name of a community situated in Lanark County, Ontario, that county being named after Lanark, Scotland.

Several places have been named after the Orkney Islands however, and one Canadian community is believed to have been named after the classical name of Orkney, Orcadia.

Orcadia, Saskatchewan was named by Scottish emigrants from the islands who, it is claimed, preferred the Latin version to the English. The name may have been influenced by the style of Nova Scotia, the Latin for New Scotland.

There are also two Orkney Springs. One is a health resort in the foothills of the Alleghenies where there are mineral springs in Shenandoah county, north west Virginia. The other is a gold mining town in the Transvaal region of South Africa on the Vaal River. The South African town has chosen the sea lion as its emblem, which relates to the meaning of its Scottish name.

Orkney, South Africa was named after a small gold mine which was worked by Scot, Simon Fraser, who came from the Orkney Islands. Many Scots fortune seekers arrived in the Transvaal region following the discovery of gold in 1862. The town was proclaimed in 1940, although Fraser's farm had been here since the 1880s.

Simon Fraser was one of Western Transvaal's pioneering gold miners and his original shaft in which he brought gold to the surface by means of a wheelbarrow is still in use today as a ventilation shaft. From these small beginnings the town now boasts the world's largest goldmine, now owned by the Vaal Reefs Exploration and Mining Company. Approximately 50,000 people have worked on the mine's ten shafts and many of the employees came from Orkney.

A major disaster struck the Vaal Reefs goldmine in Orkney on May 12, 1995 when up to a hundred miners died when a locomotive and carriage operating 1.5 miles underground fell down a shaft on top of a lift cage carrying miners.

Orkney may owe its existence to the excavation of gold but it isn't only gold that has been mined in the area. For many years diamond digging was also a prominent industry. In recent years the area has also relied heavily on the tourism industry with the creation of Orkney-Vaal Holiday Resort which offers tourist visits to the gold mines.

Inverness

Situated at the north west of the Great Glen, Inverness, Scotland is commonly referred to as the 'Capital of the Highlands'. Inverness-shire was Scotland's largest county before local government reorganisation in 1975 covering an area of 2,695,094 acres, mostly mountain peaks and glens, often filled by glistening lochs.

There is the remains of a Clava ring cairn in Inverness's Raigmore housing estate while the hill fort of Craig Phadraig show signs of ancient occupation. Inverness's eleventh century castle features in Shakespeare's Macbeth although Duncan I was unlikely to have been murdered here. The original timber castle was replaced by a stone construction on Castle Hill, which although partly destroyed by Robert I, was rebuilt in the fifteenth century and continued in use until 1746.

In 1746 the castle was taken by Prince Charles Edward Stewart and destroyed. Legend has it that the French demolition expert responsible for the destruction of the castle blew up himself and his pet dog in the process, the latter surviving minus its tail.

I tracked down eight communities throughout the world which have taken their title from the Scottish Capital of the Highlands. These include towns in Canada, New Zealand and the United States where there are five Invernesses.

The name, Inverness comes from the Scottish town's location at the mouth of the River Ness and derives from the Gaelic word 'inbhir' meaning 'river-mouth'. Ness is believed to have derived from an old Celtic word 'nesta' meaning 'roaring one'. However an American writer who lives in Inverness, Florida believed wrongly the name originated from nearby Loch Ness. He wrote, "The name 'Inverness', according to history books refers to the calm beauty of Loch Ness in Scotland."

The Florida version of Inverness is the seat of Citrus county and is situated on the west coast of central Florida on the Gulf coast. According to the local history books the city was named by a 'lonely Scotsman', who proclaimed, "It looks like Inverness, between the headlands and the lakes in Scotland. And this beautiful place deserves the name of Inverness."

The town was founded by Peter and Alf Thompkins, two confederate soldiers just after the American Civil War. The settlement was first named after its founders, Peter and Alf and became known as Thompkinsville.

A phosphate mining boom began as prospectors flooded into the area and the settlement expanded. The lonely Scot, whose name is unknown, is said to have been one of many phosphate prospectors to have arrived in this area of Florida following discovery of mineral deposits by Charles P Savary. Apparently the Scot offered to pay $2,000 to build a new courthouse if they would name the boom town in honour of his hometown, Inverness in Scotland. The name change took place in 1891.

In 1887 the county called Hernando was divided into three, creating Citrus, Pasco and Hernando counties under the orders of Senator Austin Mann who suggested that the county seat be temporarily placed at a town named Mannfield, named after himself.

Between 1889 and 1890 several elections were held to find a permanent county seat but all of them failed as there was not a significant majority. Finally in 1891 Inverness gained a majority of four votes over Lecanto and the Commission ordered that the courthouse be located in Inverness. The advocates of Mannfield were infuriated and claimed the election had been rigged. They sent a rider on horseback to Dade City where a regional judge was holding court to try to get an injunction against the move. When the messenger arrived the judge had boarded a train leaving for Tampa but the persistent rider leapt on the train and argued the case all the way to Tampa.

The citizens of Inverness however did not waste any time in grabbing the reigns of power. Just hours after the vote was counted the Inverness contingent began loading all records and furnishings for the move. A newspaper of the time reported that, "immediately upon this announcement a hundred hands began tearing down the walls of the Circuit Court Clerk's office, and loading up of county property records for removal."

Apparently even the clerk, Captain Zimmerman, who refused to move, was picked up in his chair and placed on a wagon and transported to Inverness where he was unloaded!

In 1961 the courthouse and city was used for filming Elvis Presley's first comedy film *Follow That Dream*. Many of the Inverness residents are said to recall rubbing shoulders with 'The King'.

The first industry of the Citrus county area was citrus fruit growing, but disaster struck the industry in the winter of 1894 when a hard frost wiped it out. The dead trees were rooted out to make way for cattle.

Today the Florida town has little industry other than tourism. The many lakes and rivers in the region provide opportunities for fishing, boating and diving. The population now stands at 6,462 (1993).

In 1990 the City of Inverness in Florida exchanged gifts with its namesake in Scotland when a resident of the US city was on holiday in the UK. The American visitor presented the Scots town with a wooden plaque and business card on behalf of Mayor O J Humphries.

Inverness, Nova Scotia, Canada was first known as Broad Cove until 1903. Other communities around Inverness also had their name changed to Scottish titles as Broad Cove Intervale became Strathlorne and Broad Cove Marsh changed its name to Dunvegan. They all lie in a county called Inverness which takes up the entire western half of Cape Breton Island.

The name change was suggested by Sir William Young, the community's first representative in the provincial assembly. Young was born in Inverness-shire, Scotland, naming the county after his birthplace.

Although ships had been making their way to this part of Nova Scotia since the late eighteenth century the pioneering movement did not reach the shores of Inverness until 1803. It was in this year that two Scotsmen surveyed western Cape Breton Island.

The men were not related, but one was named Donald MacIssac and the other is known as Angus MacIssac, and both originally came from the Isle of Skye. It seems to have been sheer chance. They both arrived on the same day and established their homes where Inverness county now lies and a few settlers arrived in the following years. A small quantity of coal was mined in 1867 and in the 1880s the Broad Cove area gained prominence when a coal mine was opened by William Hussey.

Hussey set up the Broad Cove Coal Company establishing the area as a coal mining centre. Many of the homes built by the coal companies still remain today. Early census and land reports record a large number of Irish living in the area, many of whom had come via Newfoundland before the Scots arrived, settling and working as schoolteachers, store accountants and craftspeople. The town of Inverness was incorporated in 1904.

There has been a decline in the population of Inverness since the1880s as the lure of metropolitan Canada and its employment opportunities has proved attractive. At the same time however others have come to Inverness, Cape Breton Island to escape the cities, seeking a quieter life. As a result almost a quarter of Inverness's residents are over the age of 65.

The Scots brought their language and culture to the area and on many parts of the island the Gaelic language, although it has diminished, is still in use today. The town of Inverness on the Island of Cape Breton in Nova Scotia, Canada has a population of 2,200 whilst the county's population stands at 18,000.

Inverness, Illinois is a north western suburb of Chicago. It is a small village thirty miles from the Chicago 'Loop' originally designed as a rural getaway for young families but has grown into one of the most exclusive residential areas in Chicago. The village was developed in 1938 by Arthur T McIntosh who named the settlement after Inverness-shire, Scotland. In 1962 after a quarter of a century of being an exclusive real estate development the community was incorporated as a village. The population of Inverness, Illinois currently stands at 1,130.

There are Invernesses elsewhere in the United States in California, Florida, Mississippi and Montana. In Canada there is a community of the same name in Quebec. There is also a small town in Jamaica named Inverness.

Lanarkshire

the town crest of Blantyre, Malawi also contains the thistle, the emblem of Scotland, to symbolise the origin of the name

The collapse of the predominant cotton industry (King Cotton) and the grinding poverty of Scottish weavers spawned a series of exiled Lanarkshire communities across the world in Canada, United States and Australia. Few of the inhabitants of Lanark in Florida, Rutherglen in Victoria, Australia or Bothwell in Ontario, Canada are probably aware of why their communities were given a Scottish title, or why all these years ago Scots left their homeland to settle in far off places.

The movement of populations is usually driven by economic or political reasons and in the case of Lanarkshire weavers in the nineteenth century it was the decline of the cotton industry and later its eventual collapse brought about by the American Civil War.

The original Lanark dates back to Roman times and owed its existence to the Roman road from Carlisle in the south. The name Lanark probably means 'clearing' or a 'slip of level ground' deriving from the Brittonic word 'Llannerch'.

Cotton manufacturing came to Lanarkshire, Scotland when David Dale founded the village of New Lanark in 1784 which of course makes it older than any of its namesakes abroad. The cotton mills were powered by the waters of the River Clyde, and despite a general decline in the industry some of the mills remained in operation until 1968.

Supplies of raw cotton to Britain were cut off in 1861 with the onset of the American Civil War. The industry had begun to decline in the 1820s. As well as the change from hand-loom to steam loom weaving, wages had fallen rapidly when women and Irish workers began to join the workforce and were often willing to work for less money.

An article appeared in the *Clydesdale Journal* on May 10th, 1820, stating that several emigrant societies had applied to the county of Lanark for aid and facilities to obtain settlements in North America. Twenty two emigration societies were formed largely aimed at assisting the emigration of weavers. During 1820 between 1,200 and 2,000 people mainly from Lanarkshire were allotted land in Ontario.

Three settlements were established in south eastern Ontario, but the settlements of Dalhousie and Ramsay did not last long and today only one survives. This was settled by the weavers in 1820 and named Lanark.

Another Lanark was established in Florida. This town was named by a renowned thread-man called William Clark who came from Lanarkshire, Scotland. It is thought that he emigrated from Scotland following the collapse of the cotton industry.

Clark arrived in the United States where he rose to become president of the Scottish Land and Improvement Company and formed the Clark Syndicate Companies. The company's business was in buying, selling and improving land and it was responsible for building the Carrabelle, Tallahassee and Georgia Railroad in 1893. Clark's Syndicate recognised the need for a hotel along the railway line so they chose the most accessible and desirable spot and called it Lanark-on-the-Gulf after Clark's hometown in Scotland. They named the streets running east to west after Board members and friends and they chose the name of the Scottish town of Paisley for the section with the best waterfront lots.

Lanark-on-the-Gulf became a popular resort due to Clark's

Syndicate having built a large hotel which they named the Lanark Inn. It had in its centre a natural spring of water twenty feet deep and was the social centre of the resort. However a series of disasters brought an end to the resort's popularity. A hurricane in 1929 destroyed the pier and bathhouses and in the early 1930s a fire destroyed the Lanark Inn. Although rebuilt, the hotel declined in popularity and only operated on a limited scale until the Second World War.

The onset of the war brought a new rather less glamorous use for Lanark-on-the-Gulf. It became Camp Gordon Johnstone, a training camp for soldiers. It was from this camp that General Omar Bradley went on to command the 2nd Army Corps in North Africa and lead the invasion of Sicily and Italy. He then went to England where he helped plan the invasion of Normandy.

When the war ended the soldiers moved out and the camp fell into disrepair until 1954, when the majority of the land and buildings was purchased by Lanark Estates, a Miami based firm. In 1955 the company surveyed the site and filed a plan for Lanark Village and work began redeveloping the former army buildings. Once the redevelopment work was completed Lanark Estate advertised them as retirement homes.

The developers claimed, "Life at Lanark Village is beautiful and satisfying and you can live for less." This attracted 500 people to Lanark, many of them Scots, attracted by the familiar name. One new lady resident had even grown up in Lanark, Scotland.

In 1956 the new villagers expressed their desire to have a say in how their village was run and the Lanark Village Association was formed. In 1960, following a petition from the Association the developers were encouraged to make some strict rules. For a time life in Lanark village must have been similar to living in the army camp. As well as living in the converted army buildings the residents had to follow strict rules laid down by the developers. No clothes were to hang out overnight and no washing was to be done on Sundays. One rule even stressed that visiting grandchildren were to remain in the village no longer than two weeks! Some retirement home! Today Lanark, Florida remains a retirement village, although grandchildren are now allowed to stay a little longer.

The railroad was also the reason why Lanark, Illinois was founded

103

in 1861. Whilst Florida's Lanark was founded as a result of the need for a hotel along the Carrabelle, Tallahassee and Georgia Railroad, thirty years previously, another Lanark sprang up in Illinois when the railroad arrived. Although in this case it was the Western Union railroad.

Among the early industries of Lanark, Illinois, was a woollen mill and carpet weaving, but it cannot be certain whether the weavers came from Lanarkshire, Scotland although it is highly possible. The town was not named from the birthplace of a settler, but by the residents in honour of the home of the Scottish bankers who funded the building of the railroad.

Indeed the first name chosen for the new town was Glasgow after the home of the 'Scottish capitalists' who backed the building of the Western Union Railroad. It was then discovered that there was already a town in Illinois of this name, so in 1859 the name was changed to Lanark, the county of Scotland's Glasgow.

Pioneer settlers had arrived in Carroll County, northern Illinois long before the railway in the 1830s and in 1844 David Becker built the first house. He was determined to build his home "away out on the prairie" although others saw this as a foolish thing to do, claiming, "no civilised white man or women could withstand the exposure and winds of an unobstructed prairie plain."

However, Becker proved them wrong and in later years he was followed by more settlers. By the 1860s the need for a railroad was crucial as the population of northern Illinois had grown. So in October 1861 the Iron Horse finally reached Lanark and within a few years the settlement had a population of 1,500.

The town became a busy shipping point for grain and livestock but there were problems. Trains frequently came off the rails and on one occasion, following a train wreck, one of the Lanark residents found himself chatting to Chief Sitting Bull. The Indian chief had strolled into town with some of the other passengers whose trains were delayed due to the wreck. Sitting Bull was on his way back from Washington DC having signed a Government treaty. Lanark is now a small town with a population of around 1,400. Many buildings from the 1880s still stand in the 'downtown'. Today one of the main industries in Lanark is a drink refrigeration plant producing over 170,000 coolers a year, which are shipped around the world.

Lanarkshire emigrants also arrived Down Under, one of them being John A Wallace who was attracted by the opportunities in the colonies. Wallace was born in Rutherglen, Lanarkshire, one of the oldest royal burghs in Scotland created around the year 1126.

In early times being a royal burgh gave Rutherglen certain rights and privileges in trading within a certain area. Whilst Lanark was the royal burgh of southern Lanarkshire, Rutherglen's trading area mainly comprised the northern half of Lanarkshire and even included Glasgow at one time.

During his reign, King David I of Scotland created a number of burghs to encourage trade throughout his kingdom. There is no doubt, however, that Rutherglen was a busy trade centre prior to this. It is likely to have been in existence as early as the sixth century when it was said to have been the only town of commercial importance between Lanark and Ayr.

Advertisements in local papers offered "free grants of land" in Canada and "free passages to Australia" to all whose trades were in demand in the colonies. Such copy appeared in the *Hamilton Advertiser* on November 29th, 1861, encouraging Scots to emigrate. It read, "Why cling on to one poor spot like limpets to the rocks, and starve, and fight, and tear the bite out of each other's mouths when the wide world invites our enterprise, and offers ample room and rations for us all. Canada and our other colonies offer splendid fields."

John Wallace migrated from his native Rutherglen in the 1860s to Victoria, Australia during the gold rush, where he opened up a chain of hotels in various goldfields. When John Wallace arrived at Wahgunyah where the Australian Rutherglen now stands he soon realized that the settlement was likely to develop and laid out the township site, leaving the prime corner block for himself, where he erected the Star Hotel.

The settlement was named over a round of drinks when a David Hamilton, himself a Scot, from Glasgow said to Wallace, "John, if you are prepared to shout the bar when you open the Star, you can call it after your native town."

Wallace replied, "Right you are Davie. Rutherglen it will be!"

The first specks of gold in what was to become the Wahgunyah Rush had been found in the spring of 1860. Gold seekers came from all over to Rutherglen and within six months an estimated 15,000

John Wallace, a native of Rutherglen, Lanarkshire
who emigrated to Austraia and set up a chain of hotels during a
gold rush and who named Rutherglen, Victoria, Australia
Courtesy Rutherglen Museum, Scotland

people were on the goldfields of Wahgunyah. David Glen Hamilton had arrived on the fields within one week of the first gold with a ten-bullock dray of goods for sale to the prospectors. He and his brother William had arrived in Victoria in 1851, and after a short try at the goldfields went into business as general merchants and suppliers.

Many stories are told of the exodus from Melbourne to the goldfields and of the ships left in port without crews as seamen left to search for gold. To cater for the sudden rush twenty one licensed hotels and many unlicensed 'grog shops' opened as places of amusement. Many had dancing saloons although it was estimated men outnumbered women twenty to one! In a bid to balance out the sexes cartloads of women were brought from Melbourne, many of them immigrant girls, who on arrival in Australia were anxious to reach the goldfields and find jobs without understanding what they were doing or where they were going.

In their new 'homes' their household duties were light, but at night they were expected to dance – they usually did – for if they refused they would be cast out. The girls soon discovered that the men wanted partners for life and many of them married and settled down almost as fast as they were brought in!

Sadly, little is known of the first inhabitants of the Rutherglen district, the Aborigines, but it is said that between four and six tribes roamed the area, each with two or three hundred members. By 1863, just three years after gold was discovered in the area it was estimated that only seventy two of these early inhabitants survived.

Thirty thousand prospectors tried their luck in the Rutherglen goldfields. The yield of gold reached its peak in 1897 when 61,480ozs were won. The last goldfield closed down in the 1980s and today Rutherglen is better known for its wines rather than its mines. Thirteen wineries are now a major employer as well as being a tourist attraction. One of them, 'Clydeside Cellars' was named by David Hamilton in the late 1800s.

Today the largest employer is Uncle Toby's, a producer of cereal and health foods and the shire is also a major agricultural area, mainly in sheep, cattle and grain production and Rutherglen's population now stands at around 2,250. In 1911 young and old Rutherglen were brought together when an exchange of flags took place between the school children of Rutherglen, Australia and Rutherglen, Scotland.

Although John Wallace never returned to Scotland before his death in 1901, he is remembered in the history book *Rutherglen Lore* by W Ross Shearer. Shearer says, "Probably no Ruglonian will ever attain to higher distinction in the estimation of a people than did the late Hon J A Wallace, the great gold mining speculator of Victoria, Australia."

Another settlement to be named after a Lanarkshire town is Bothwell, Ontario. This Canadian town owes its success to the discovery of 'black gold' by Samuel Smith as he surveyed the area in the mid nineteenth century. The oil wells however led to some confusion among the Canadian town's people about how their town was named. Some believe the name Bothwell comes from the words 'both wells'. Others, while accepting the fact that their town has been named after Bothwell, Scotland believe that the Scottish town derives its name from 'Archibald the Grim'!

A history book of the Canadian town *Black Gold Built Bothwell* recounts how when Archibald the Grim built Bothwell Church in Scotland in 1398, arrows fired by two archers fell side by side. Thus says the book, the name comes from his expression 'Both well shot'!

The true meaning of Bothwell is not quite as romantic. The name derives from the old English words, 'both' meaning 'hut', and 'well' meaning 'pool', meaning 'the hut near the pool'.

The Ontario town was given its name by Canadian politician George Brown after the birthplace of his mother. George Brown was born the son of a city merchant in Edinburgh, Scotland in 1818. He emigrated with his father in 1838 to New York and later moved on to Toronto, where in 1844 he founded the *Toronto Globe and Mail* newspaper. This newspaper became known as 'the Scotsman's Bible' as it reflected the radical opposition and the puritanical morality strong among the Scots.

Bothwell was founded in 1854, after George Brown acquired 4,000 acres of land in Toronto. One of the town's claim to fame is that he actually laid out the town and had it incorporated before there were any settlers! Brown began to advertise in his newspaper, *The Globe*, for settlers to go to Bothwell, but many of the first settlers were his own employees who were mechanics he had brought from Scotland.

Brown's political career began in 1851 when he entered the Canadian House and he later became a Canadian Minister. On 27th

June 1867 Brown called the Reform Convention which established Confederation thus forming modern day Canada. To this day George Brown is remembered as the Father of Confederation. Unfortunately at the first General Election after Confederation he was defeated in the running for South Ontario by Mr T N Gibbs.

From then on he devoted his energies to his newspaper until tragically, on 25th March 1880 he was shot by a former employee called Bennett, who had been discharged from work for 'irregular habits'. Bennet had gone into Brown's office with a revolver with the intention of intimidating him, but Brown was shot in the leg as he struggled with Bennett and died less than six weeks later on May 9th. Before his tragic death, Brown had seen his settlement grow into a town of over 3,500.

The population exploded when John Lick struck oil on April Fools' Day in 1863. It was no joke however. Oil speculators flocked into the area hoping to get rich, because at one time the well was earning $10,000 a day! John Lick was said to have been offered $500,000 for his oil well and local folklore says he was even offered a wheelbarrow full of gold for the well. Two hundred and three oil wells were drilled in the area but by 1866, just three years after the first oil gushed from the Lick well, only thirty one of these remained in business. As the oil ran dry, Bothwell's population dwindled and today it stands at little over 800. However, some of the original oil wells are still being pumped in Bothwell, as a tourist attraction.

The city of Airdrie, Alberta owes its existence to the building of the TransCanada and Canadian Pacific Railway line, and William McKenzie, a CPR engineer named the station after the town in his native Scotland. In North America the railroads were generally not built to connect existing towns but to open up new areas of the country for settlers. By the 1890s all of the best land in Ontario and the United States had been occupied, so with the completion of the TransCanada railroad in 1886 Western Canada was available for settlement.

Then in 1891 the Canadian Pacific Railway completed a line from Calgary to Edmonton, passing through where Airdrie stands today. The first settlers in what is now Airdrie were employees of the CPR. Trains in the nineteenth century were unable to travel for long distances without refuelling with coal and water, so it was necessary to build stations at regular intervals and many towns were founded as a result of this.

Airdrie, being only nineteen miles from the former Calgary city limits, fitted into the railroad's programme of building stations at ten mile intervals along the route. And with an adequate supply of nonalkaline water for the steam engines at nearby Nose Creek, the CPR chose the site for a station.

The very first settlers to arrive in the region came by covered wagon and established farms and ranches in the area and Airdrie remains proud of its farming and ranching history. Every year cowboys from throughout North America take part in Airdrie's three day Annual Rodeo and Canada Day Parade. Ranching is one of the four symbols identifiable on the Canadian city's crest. The four symbols are a tribute to the cornerstones of Airdrie's economy and include oil and gas, livestock, cropfarming and manufacturing industries.

The Canadian city took its name from Scotland's Airdrie which stands on land given to the Cistercian monks of Newbattle Abbey by Malcolm IV around the year 1161. But it is believed that the first residents were Celts or Gauls who inhabited this part of Scotland in ancient times. Hence the Gaelic name Airdrie – 'ArdRuighe' means 'high slope'.

In 1695 an Act of Parliament granted a charter making Airdrie, Scotland a market town with the townsfolk engaged in weaving, distilling, brewing and candle making.

When created a Burgh of Barony in 1821 the town quickly grew in size and industry, but since 1975 Airdrie has been joined with the neighbouring town of Coatbridge and part of the county of Lanarkshire to form Monklands District. In 1996 after further local government reform the town now makes up part of North Lanarkshire Council.

The ancient Scottish burgh has developed close links with its sister town in Alberta. Both communities have kept in touch through the formation of a Twinning Committee in recent years.

There are several other towns in the world with Lanarkshire names including Blantyre, Malawi; Cathkin Peak in South Africa; Lanark, West Virginia, USA. Rutherglen in Ontario, Canada was named by a native of the Scottish town when he worked on the CPR railroad. There are also Rutherglens in Tasmania and New Zealand.

There are also a staggering thirty six towns bearing the name of Lanarkshire's county town, Hamilton. Although many of these have been named after surnames of settlers, there is no doubt some have taken their title from the Scots town. In addition there is a Cape Hamilton, Fort Hamilton, Lake Hamilton, Mount Hamilton, Hamilton Acres, Hamilton Air Force Base, Hamilton Beach, Hamilton Cove, Hamilton Dam, Hamilton Field, Hamilton Inlet and a town called Hamilton Lakes.

Lothian

Midlothian, Illinois — the village crest contains the lion rampant and thistles

There are three Lothians in Scotland, East, West and Mid, with the capital of Scotland, Edinburgh being within Midlothian.

Even though Midlothian, Illinois was named after the Scottish Midlothian some may believe the residents of the American town have gone overboard with their Scottish connections. Looking at the official letterhead of the village you could be forgiven for believing it was the town seal of an ancient Scottish burgh. The Scottish lion rampant appears in the centre of the town seal surrounded by thistles and tartan.

The Midlothian, Illinois village was established in 1898 when a group of wealthy Chicago tycoons decided to locate their new golf course there. The club was one of the first three in the Chicago area. With golf being a Scottish game the country club chose the name 'Midlothian' from Walter Scott's novel *The Heart of Midlothian*.

Around the turn of the century the golf club members decided that they needed a faster mode of transport to their new club and a spur track was built so that trains could transport them to the club.

By 1915 real estate agents were becoming interested in the land surrounding the golf club for building houses. Nine years later the Midlothian Development Association was formed with the idea of establishing a village and three years later Midlothian was incorporated.

For several years the Midlothian Highland Games were an annual event in the village. Scottish and American athletes took part in the games which included caber tossing and clackner throwing. The Highland games are now held elsewhere in Chicago. However the golf course is still in use today located to the west of the village. The population has increased to around 15,000 but the village remains a residential community with no major industry.

Even though the village of Gifford in East Lothian, Scotland is barely two hundred years old there are at least five places in the United States that bear the same name. The Scottish village was named after the Gifford family who had owned the land in the area centuries previously. Gifford's namesakes include one in Florida, Iowa, Washington, Missouri and South Carolina.

Dunbar means fort on the hill derived from the Gaelic 'dun' meaning 'hill' or 'fortress' and 'barr' meaning 'height'. Six communities in the United States have adopted the name Dunbar after the Lothian town. They are in Nebraska, Utah, Wisconsin, Pennsylvania, Kansas and Oklahoma, plus Dunbar in Queensland, Australia.

The industrial town Bathgate, located in West Lothian, was given by Robert I to his daughter Marjorie on her wedding to Walter the High Steward in 1316.

Situated on the Glasgow–Edinburgh road the town became a centre for handloom weaving. Coal and shale mining took over and in 1850 James 'Paraffin' Young opened his first paraffin refinery here.

There are two possibilities as to where the name Bathgate derives. The first suggests that the name means 'house in the woods' from the Brittonic words 'both' meaning 'house' and 'cett' meaning 'wood'. Others suggest that the name means 'boar woods' from the Brittonic word 'baedd' which means 'boar'. Bathgate, North Dakota is the only town to have been named after the Scottish community in West Lothian.

Until the mid nineteenth century Leith was Scotland's principal port with connections to France, the Baltic and America, dealing in grain, sugar, flax, iron, paper, timber and whisky. The Scottish port has inspired settlers to name areas around the world. There are five Leiths in the United States and one in Canada. They are in Ontario, Canada and in Alabama, Arkansas, Nevada, North Dakota and Georgia, USA.

There is a suburb of the city of Dunedin called Leith Valley. Dunedin itself was named after the Scots capital, as were its street names and various suburbs. Residential districts of Dunedin include Corstorphine, Musselburgh and Portobello.

Perth

the crest of Perth, Western Australia incorporates that of Perth, Scotland

Perth claims to be Scotland's ancient capital and also uses the title city. However this claim is questionable as it has never had a cathedral. Perth's claim to be the ancient capital in reality relates to its proximity to Scone where Scottish monarchs were crowned.

No one can be quite certain where Perth derived its name. One suggestion is that the name comes from the Brittonic word 'pert' meaning 'thicket' while the more likely origin is the city's position on the River Tay and comes from the words 'aber' meaning 'at the mouth of' and Tay, this being shortened to 'Bertha', a Roman fort which stood two miles to the north. Perth has also been referred to as St John's Town, St John's being the great church of St John the Baptist. This was shortened to St Johnstone a name that is still used for Perth's football club. On 11th May 1559 St John's church was the setting for John Knox's sermon which sparked off the Reformation throughout Scotland. No one may be certain as to how Perth, Scotland came to be named. But one thing is certain – the Scottish town gave its name to seventeen other Perths throughout the world.

One of the most well-known Scottish named towns abroad is Perth, Western Australia, a city of over one million inhabitants. Its Scottish namesake has little over 40,000. It is hard to believe perhaps, that while Perth, Scotland has been around since Roman times, its sister city in Western Australia was born in 1829 – less than two hundred years ago.

Skyscrapers overshadow the streets of the Aussie city and a brochure on the Australian city says, "While the buildings of its Scottish namesake huddle together as if for warmth, the Antipodean city spreads itself out on the cooling rim of river, sea and park."

There was much controversy when the Australian settlement was named Perth. Lieutenant James Stirling who had dreamt up the idea of a settlement in Western Australia suggested in 1827 that the colony be given a poetic name such as Hesperia, meaning towards the west. The Lieutenant was furious when the Colonial Secretary was adamant that the settlement be named after his home town of Perth.

The name also outraged many colonists, one of whom wrote to Westminster on no less than six occasions blasting that the town had been named after an ". . . . insignificant place known only to reading men, or to geographers, as an obscure place in Scotland. Who ever heard of it?"

Inhabitants of Perth, Scotland will no doubt object to being described as a 'hubble of buildings' or as being obscure. It is after all on the magnificent River Tay and is the world headquarters of General Accident Fire and Life Insurance Company as well as being the home to Bells Whisky.

The first European to visit Perth, Australia was Dutch navigator William de Vlamingh who explored the Swan River in 1697. It was not until 1827 when Lieutenant James Stirling made an unscheduled visit to the area that there was any attempt to settle western Australia. Stirling returned to Sydney full of enthusiasm for the establishment of a settlement of free colonists but it was only after eighteen months of persuasion that John Barrow, secretary for the Admiralty, was convinced. He had just heard that the French were planning a penal colony on the west coast of New Holland, the early title of Western Australia.

In February 1829 the *Parmelia* set sail with HMS *Sulphur* carrying fifty five free settlers bound for the Swan River in western Australia named after the black swans found there. Eighteen ships arrived in that year carrying a total of 1,868 passengers. The Swan River colony was unique in that it was settled by free colonists and not established as a penal colony.

However at first progress of the new settlement was slow and in 1850 to boost the population the settlers requested the British Government establish a penal station near Perth, at a time when other Australian colonies were trying to phase out transportation. The early settlers looked upon the convicts as a source of free labour, and when they began arriving in 1850 they assisted the building of many roads, bridges and buildings such as the Town Hall (1867-70), the Government House (1859-64) and The Cloisters.

Convicts continued to arrive at Perth until 1868 but it was the discovery of gold in the early 1890s which sparked off a population explosion. Although the gold rushes in Western Australia came late compared to Victoria and New South Wales, the effects were as dramatic and in the fifteen years between 1890 and 1905 the population of the Western Australian town rocketed from 48,502 to over 250,000.

A twentieth century 'rush' came in the 1960s, this time brought about by the discovery of precious minerals such as iron ore and nickel. Instead of the saloons and dancing halls built during the gold rush, the sixties boom changed the skyline of Perth as skyscrapers sprang up.

Despite the early opposition to be named after an "obscure huddle of buildings" in Scotland the relationship between the two cities has flourished. While researching material for this book Jan Watt, PR manager at the City of Perth, Council House, told me, "The connection between the two Perths has been sustained over the years, enhanced from time to time by the visits to Western Australia by the Provost of Perth, Scotland and by visits to Scotland by our Lord Mayor and other Council representatives."

Residents of both cities often exchange visits and one Australian resident found himself speaking to his friends and relatives of his hometown via the radio while visiting Perth, Scotland. Pilot officer Roy Cannaway was on leave in the Scots city when a special broadcast was made to Perth, Western Australia by the then Lord Provost Robert Nimmo on April 10th 1943.

When asked to tell the residents of Australia what he thought of Perth, Scotland Roy Cannaway said, "Well, after our spacious and sunny city with its tree shaded streets, wide verandahs and large modern buildings, Perth, Scotland, gives me the impression of being a little cramped, somewhat sombre and may be described as somewhat grimy."

However the cheerful Australian added, "I certainly admire your two grand public parks – the North and South Inches. I could not understand why they got that name, because they seemed miles long and broad to me."

He also explained that he could find no trace of the black swans that had been presented to the Scottish city in 1937 when Lord Mayor Poynton visited Scotland in 1937. The black swan is a symbol of Perth, Australia and appears on the city's crest which was amended in 1949 to bear the official shield of Perth, Scotland.

On the opposite side of Australia lies Scone in New South Wales which was named after Scone, Perthshire, Scotland, the ancient site where Scotland's Kings and Queens were crowned. Scone, near Perth, became Scotland's capital around 840AD. Legend has it that the Stone of Destiny was brought to Scone in the ninth century from the Middle East and used as part of the enthronement ceremony of Scottish monarchs.

It is claimed that it was a pillow used by Jacob in Biblical times but Scots author Sir Compton Mackenzie believed that it had been quarried near Oban in the west Highlands of Scotland. Others believe that the stone was brought to Scone by Kenneth I, the 36th king of Dalriada, who transferred his seat to Scone to prevent further Viking raids. According to legend the stone embodied the blessing of St Patrick which stated that wherever the stone lay the race of Erc should reign.

However the Stone of Destiny, also known as the Stone of Scone was removed to England by Edward I in 1296. The stone, which is sandstone and is 26 inches long, 16 inches wide and 11 inches high, weighs 336lbs. Its only decoration is a Latin cross and it now lies in Westminster Abbey underneath the coronation throne.

In 1950 an attempt was made to return the Stone to its rightful resting place at Scone when on Christmas morning that year Scottish nationalists removed it. However it was repossessed by the English after being placed in Arbroath Abbey. Today Scone, Scotland is a small rural community with 4,500 inhabitants.

The village of Scone in New South Wales was named after the ancient Scottish crowning place when two old Scots soldiers began talking of the importance of having a place prepared so that in the event of a major disaster the coronation stone may be appropriately housed. The elderly Scots soldiers were Thomas Livingstone Mitchell who had become surveyor general of New South Wales and Hugh Cameron, a farmer who both settled in the area in 1828.

One day Mitchell visited his old friend Cameron who took out a petition reading, "As this valley of the Kingdom Ponds has not received a general name, that it might be called Strathearne" after the valley close to Scone Palace in Perthshire, Scotland. Cameron's farm became known as Strathearn and the nearby village was renamed Scone.

Another Australian town to be named after the Perthshire area of Scotland is Dunkeld in Victoria, which like Scone, owes its existence to Major Thomas Mitchell. Although the Dunkeld area had been occupied by the Tchapwurong people for over 40,000 years the first white settlers arrived in Dunkeld, Victoria in 1836. Surveyor General of New South Wales Major Thomas Mitchell led a party who travelled through the area and camped at the spot where Dunkeld now lies. Settlers quickly followed but sadly, their arrival brought about a rapid and disastrous collapse of the native population.

At first Dunkeld was called Mount Sturgeon but early Scottish settlers said that the mountains, which were called the Grampians after the mountain region in Scotland, reminded them of home. So they asked the government to change the name to Dunkeld after the Scottish village in Perthshire which Kenneth I had adopted as the capital of his kingdom along with Scone. The settlement took the name of Dunkeld on 1st January 1854.

In Scotland, Dunkeld lies on the River Tay fourteen miles north of Perth. The Scottish town is thought to have been founded when St Columba or St Adamnan founded the first monastery. The name Dunkeld derives from the Gaelic 'dun' meaning 'hill or fort' and 'Chailleann' meaning 'Caledonians' therefore meaning 'Fort of the Caledonians'.

Modern Dunkeld consists of only two main streets as the original town was burnt to the ground in 1689 when Highlanders loyal to the Crown descended upon the Covenanting Cameronians who held it. Much of the town has been restored by the National Trust for Scotland and it is now a picturesque village with around 1300 residents.

The first settlers arrived in Dunkeld, Victoria in 1839, with more arriving in the early 1840s and during the gold rushes of the 1860s more settlers arrived. The roads were busy and five hotels sprang up to supply the miners. One of the hotels, which opened in 1845 was called the Woolpack Inn which was owned by Andrew Templeton. His brother James Templeton came to a tragic death at the age of just 28 years. One of the guests, a gold miner returning from the diggings shot him dead in the hotel. Apparently the man had a great deal of money and a great deal of fear that he was going to be molested. He fired through the bedroom door wounding Templeton. At day break the man escaped through an open window.

For several years the Rechabites tried to counter the effects of alcohol but it was the arrival of the railroad in 1877 that finally led to the closure of all but one of the hotels along the highway.

It was the 23rd of April that saw the official opening of the Ararat-Dunkeld line. A special train was laid on which brought Members of Parliament and other dignitaries for a ceremony and dinner held in the Railway Hotel. On its return journey to Melbourne it is said that an enterprising aboriginal put on a guard's uniform and collected a fare from all the passengers who were all in very high spirits following the celebrations. Later that year another section of railroad was opened between Dunkeld and nearby Hamilton.

In later years Dunkeld, Victoria formed reciprocal arrangements between the schools and golf clubs of Dunkeld, Scotland.

International Perthshire connections are not confined to Australia. In South Africa there is Kinross village. A G Meyer, chief executive of Kinross, South Africa told me, "I am not aware of any continued connection with Scotland, apart from Glenfiddich and Bells which is highly appreciated here."

Kinross in South Africa lies in the Transvaal region 140 kilometres east of Johannesburg and it is said to lie on the watershed between the Atlantic and Indian Oceans. It was named by the Patterson brothers who surveyed the railway line between Springs and Bethal between 1904 and 1906. It is believed that they came from Kinross,

Scotland and that they also named other railroad sidings such as Leslie and Oban.

Kinross, South Africa is surrounded by coal and gold mines and many local farmers concentrate on producing wool, potatoes and maize, but the main employers in the area are the Sasol plant which produces oil from coal.

Kinross expanded in 1980 when 350 homes were built to house employees of the Sasol plant and in 1992 a further 350 were built due to expansion of the industry. The population stood at 5,600 in 1992.

In Scotland Kinross is a small town which lies on the western shores of Loch Leven opposite Loch Leven Castle in which Mary Queen of Scots was imprisoned. The name stands for 'at the head of the cape' and derives from the Gaelic words 'cinn' meaning 'at the head' and 'ros' meaning 'cape'.

In Canada there are two Perths. It is curious but true that only a few miles away from the town of Perth in Lanark County, Ontario, there is a town called Lanark in Perth County!

Perth, Ontario lies on the banks of the Tay River which was named by early settlers in the area. The river is joined to a network of canals which provide access to around thirty lakes. The canals were built between 1831 and 1834 by the Tay Navigation Company.

Perth, Ontario was founded in 1816 by the British military and lowland Scots as a reserve for disbanded troops from the War of 1812-14 and loyal Scottish settlers many of whom were stonemasons. This surely explains the impressive architecture of some of Perth's buildings.

After the war military strategists placed settlements fifty miles from the United States border and encouraged residence by former military troops and immigrants from Scotland who could be rallied to repel any aggressive move from the United States. The town is situated in eastern Ontario not far from the capital, Ottawa and was for a time the administration centre for Ontario.

Today the Canadian town has a population of around 6,600 and one of its claims to fame is that it is the site of Canada's last ever fatal duel. The local museum displays the pistols used in the duel which took place in 1833. The loser was Robert Lyon who fought to defend the honour of his girlfriend, schoolteacher and local governess, Elizabeth Hughes. The first time the two men, who were both law students, turned around and fired both missed their target. They were prepared to call it a day but Lyon's second insisted that the duel continue. The pair reloaded their guns, took twelve paces, turned around and as the guns fired Lyon dropped dead. What Lyon didn't know was that his second had a crush on Hughes and wanted her for himself. With friends like that who needs enemies!

There are several Perths in the United States including those in Kansas, New York, North Dakota and Indiana. Also in the United States is Perthshire, Mississippi and Perth Amboy in New Jersey. The latter was settled in 1683 and later incorporated in 1718. It is a harbour at the mouth of the Raritan River and was a shipbuilding region for some time.

Other spots bearing the title Perth include Perth, Tasmania. There is also Perth Water Bay and a Perth Water which flows into the Swan River in Western Australia and a town called Perthville in New South Wales. Another Perth is in British Guiana.

Other communities names after Perthshire placenames include Kinloch, Saskatchewan and a town of the same name in Missouri. The latter was settled by a Scottish famliy and named after their native village near Blairgowrie in Scotland.

Renfrew

The name Renfrew derives from the old Brittonic words 'rhyn' meaning 'point' and 'frwd' meaning 'stream'. The name 'point of the stream' refers to the rivers Clyde and Gryfe which come together here.

The only other town to be named Renfrew lies in Ontario, Canada and is the seat of a county of the same name. The first settlers were a mixture of Scottish and Irish, but the Scots got their way as far as naming the town and county of Renfrew was concerned.

The first visitors in the Renfrew area of Ontario were fur traders and lumbermen who had to travel along the river by canoe. The first recorded settler was a lumber jobber named Joseph Brunette who arrived in 1823 and cleared around thirty of the 200 acres of land he had claimed and built his home there before he died in 1832.

In 1825 a second settler arrived, Thomas McLean, but he did not stay in the area long. Although McLean intended to settle on the land granted to his brother for service in the British Army, his first crops failed and he returned to the town of Perth in Lanark County, Ontario.

But the land was not left abandoned as McLean rented 200 acres to Sergeant Henry Airth who was fleeing McNab Township, a settlement that had been established when the Highland chief, the Laird of McNab brought over a party of settlers from Scotland and tried to re-establish the old feudal system in the New World. The rest of McLean's land was rented out to Joseph Mayhew, and in 1829 both men arrived with their families making up most of Renfrew's population of 21.

In the following years more people arrived but by 1840 there were still only 42 Renfrew inhabitants. However in the mid 1850s there was an influx of settlers when the government sponsored the building of the Opeongo Line, a colonisation road following the watersheds of the Madawaska and Bonnechere Rivers, part of which became Renfrew's main street.

In 1858 Renfrew had enough inhabitants to break away from neighbouring Horton Township and it became a village, adopting the motto 'Let Renfrew Flourish', which may have come from emigrants from Glasgow, Scotland whose city crest carries this motto. The Scottish connotation lies not only in the words but in the thistles which surround the motto.

Today the descendants of these Scots pioneers continue to keep the Scottish traditions and customs alive in Renfrew, Ontario. Although the identity of the person that named Renfrew has now been forgotten, there is no doubt that it was named either after the Scots town of Renfrew or after the county of Renfrewshire. There are organisations such as the Renfrew Thistle Club, a group of Scottish descent who arrange St Andrew's Night and Burns Night events, and the Lanark & Renfrew pipe band. At one time Renfrew, Ontario even held its very own Highland games each year!

These are not the only links between the Ontario town and its namesake in Scotland. In 1920, when the twelfth century Paisley Abbey, in Paisley, Scotland was under restoration the kind citizens of Renfrew, Ontario donated a substantial sum of money.

Ontario's connection with Renfrewshire is also seen in the town of Paisley which was founded by Scotsman, Simon Orchard and his family who left the town of Durham, Ontario with the intention of settling but with no particular place in mind. According to local folklore Orchard built a raft of cedar logs after having a dream of "rich lands at the confluence of a river" in early Spring of 1851.

He and his family drifted down the Saugeen River in Ontario on their raft,with no idea where they would land, but by sheer chance on the very first night of their journey they made camp along the bank of the Saugeen River where it met the Teeswater River.

When daylight arrived Orchard decided that this was the place he had dreamt of and he built Paisley's very first home using the cedar logs from his raft.

A few weeks later the Orchard family were joined by Samuel Rowe, who also came from Durham, Ontario and settled on the opposite side of the river from the Orchards. The two sets of pioneers built a bridge over the Saugeen river to connect their homes but unfortunately, very high water in June 1851 carried away the fragile footbridge and the only communication between the two families was by means of a dog!

The dog, aptly named Danger, carried messages and parcels back and forth across the swollen river allowing the families to maintain contact. By 1855 the surrounding area had been snapped up by settlers at the Land Sale in nearby Southampton, and the following year Orchard and Rowe obtained a patent from the Crown and the village was surveyed.

In 1856 Thomas Orchard opened a post office and became its postmaster around which time the village became officially known as Paisley. Progress for the young Paisley was boosted further when in June 1872 the first train service was introduced and within a year the town had over 1,000 inhabitants.

Among Paisley, Ontario's first industries were two woollen mills and a foundry which made farming tools. In 1874 Paisley was organised into a separate municipality and that same year it appears that a circus came to town.

A W H Reed from Winnipeg, Manitoba recalled in the *Paisley Advocate*, the first 'circus' he had ever witnessed was in 1874 in Paisley. The residents' suspicion should have been aroused by the absence of elephants, horses, high wire acts and clowns. The circus could not even boast a lion or a tiger.

Indeed the circus top was empty apart from a rhinoceros which was chained to the centre of the ring. As Paisley's residents packed the tent the rhino broke loose causing a stampede to the tent's only exit. The red-faced citizens later learned that the incident was created by the circus employees to give the pickpockets placed in the crowd easy pickings in the crush to the exit. Many of the Paisley folk discovered that their wallets and purses had gone missing in the mayhem as the terrified residents tried to escape the rhino.

By the turn of the century the population of Paisley had grown to around 1900 people, but later the settlement declined as industries failed and residents headed west. The population plummeted to around 700, and even today lies at little more than 900.

Some 1500 miles to the west of Paisley, Ontario lies another town of the same name in Oregon, USA. This small ranching community is situated in the centre of Lake County, Oregon on the Chewaucan river 4,550 feet above sea level.

Paisley Oregon's first name was Chewaucan, similar to the river. The name, given to the area by the local Indians, means 'small potato'! The present name of the town is generally thought to have been suggested by Charles L Mitchell-Innes, a Scot who was in partnership in a general store with Paisley's first postmaster. Innes, like many of the first settlers of Paisley, Oregon was a rancher, but he was also in a partnership in a general store with Paisley's first postmaster, Samuel Steele.

Ranching was the first industry of the Oregon village and remains to this day although for some time logging and timber provided a major part of Paisley's economy.

There is also a settlement called Paisley near Lanark Village in Florida. The name Paisley was chosen for the beach front section of Lanark-on-the-Gulf in the late eighteenth century.

In Alberta, Canada, the town of Barrhead was first settled by a group under the leadership of an Anglican Church missionary, Reverend W L S Dallas who formed the first Co-operative Association and store on the site that is now considered Old Barrhead.

A Scottish journalist wrote of the Canadian town, "Barrhead was named by an immigrant Scot. As a boy of just nine years, a Mr Taylor left Barrhead for Canada in 1905 and founded with other weary pioneers the hamlet of Barrhead."

However a Canadian author, whilst writing the history of Alberta's Barrhead commented, "As a writer of long standing, I have always refrained from any criticism of the work of another author or journalist, but I must state that the Scottish journalist must have been misinformed somewhere along the trail between his or her typewriter and the source of information."

Apparently it was the directors of the Co-operative who in 1914 decided that the settlement required a name. Each director was asked to submit a name for the post office and village to the authorities in Ottawa, and of the names, Barrhead was chosen. It had been suggested by James McGuire who had emigrated from Barrhead, Scotland.

The original Barrhead in the Levern Valley, Renfrewshire, Scotland remained a small hamlet until adjoining the larger Paisley in the middle of the eighteenth century when the industrial revolution came to Scotland.

It was discovered that the Levern Valley area was ideal for the flax bleaching process. A bleach works was founded in the valley and later, in 1718 Scotland's second cotton mill, the Levern Mill was formed. By the 1830s there were a series of cotton mills, bleach fields and calico print fields along the Levern, which subsequently formed Barrhead.

Renfrew Scotland became renowned for its textile and weaving industry which was established as a cottage based industry employing many of Renfrewshire's villagers as far back as the late seventeenth century. By the 1780s Paisley's weaving industry was at its peak, employing close to a staggering seventy per cent of the town's population of 17,000 people.

At the turn of the nineteenth century the manufacturing of the Paisley Shawl began, the demand for which fluctuated as fashions changed. Paisley, which had established itself as the leading production centre of the shawls in Britain, suffered greatly when the decline of the shawl industry brought about the demise of weaving in the 1870s.

In the 1820s a group of Renfrewshire weavers joined distressed weavers from Lanarkshire, Scotland and emigrated to Canada where they were allotted land and established settlements called Dalhousie, Ramsay, and Lanark, the only one of these towns that survives today.

A group of Renfrewshire weavers settled in New York's Greenwich Village at the beginning of the nineteenth century and called their home Paisley Place. Other Renfrewshire placenames throughout the world include Paisley Seapeak in the Mozambique Channel; Paisley Pond in Oklahoma, USA; and Johnstone, Ontario, Canada.

Stirlingshire

the town crest of Arnprior, Ontario contains the lion rampant in the top left quadrant to symbolise the Scottish origins

"FORTIS ET FIDUS" - BRAVE AND FAITHFUL

There is an abundance of evidence of the migration from Stirlingshire in Scotland with four Alvas, two Bannockburns and around ten Stirlings dotted around the globe.

Many of the emigrants from the Stirlingshire region were farmers who were encouraged to leave following the disastrous harvest of 1782-83 and later, when the Corn Laws were repealed in 1846. The repeal of the Corn Laws meant financial ruin for many Scots farmers who up until then had been protected from foreign competition.

Later in the century the price of cattle suffered similarly when New Zealand and South America began to import beef and mutton cheaper. Many farmers turned to emigration societies for assistance. Evidence of the flight from the land can be seen in the advertisement placed by the Government's emigration office in the *Clydesdale Journal* on May 11th 1861 offering free passage to Victoria and Queensland for Scottish farm servants.

Stirling, Scotland, which is known as the 'Gateway to the

Highlands' was the crowning place of Mary Queen of Scots in 1543 when she was just nine years old. The name Stirling probably means 'land by the stream' derived from the Gaelic words 'sruth' meaning 'stream' and 'lann' meaning 'land'.

But the truth is that many of the towns worldwide that are named Stirling do not take their title from the Scots city, but after people. For example, Stirling in New Jersey was named after William Alexander, who succeeded his father as surveyor general and was known as Lord Stirling.

Stirling, Alberta was named after J A Stirling, managing director of The Trusts, Executors and Securities Corporation of London, England, a shareholder in the Alberta Coal and Railway Co.

But the industrial town of Stirling City in California must be unique as it is the only town I have come across to be named after a boiler! The unincorporated company town of Stirling City was established and owned by the Diamond Match sawmill company. The sawmill, which was the largest of its kind in California, had an engine room measuring sixty by forty feet, powered by a 1,200 horsepower engine. A series of huge boilers were used to generate enough steam to drive the massive engine. Each of the boilers had the name 'Stirling Consolidated' stamped across its front and this is where the town's Stirling title emanated from.

There has been little written about Stirling City but its history begins in 1901 when Diamond Match first attempted to establish a company town. In 1903 the company brought around thirty carpenters to the town to build the sawmill and various other buildings. The main industry of Stirling City, which lies in the foothills of the Sierra Nevada was the match factory.

The town of Alva, Florida is another example of a town that despite having the name of a Scottish village, has no connection that can be traced. Alva is named after a native flower of Denmark! Alva was named by a Danish seaman, captain Peter Nelson in the 1880s when he purchased land and planned to build the town of his dreams.

Captain Nelson, claimed to be the illegitimate son of the King of Denmark and to have taken what he called his fair share of the crown jewels before setting sail for Florida in 1867. When he arrived on the banks of the Caloosahatchee he noticed many white flowers growing in the area that reminded him of a bloom called Alva that grew in Denmark.

The Canadian community of Callander in Ontario, named after the Stirlingshire village has an unusual claim to fame. Like many towns it began life with the arrival of the railroad. In the beginning Callander had a prominent lumber industry and sawmill which remained in operation for many years. Fishing was carried out on Lake Nipissing but both these industries suffered greatly during the 1930s depression years and the sawmills shut down.

However on May 28th 1934 Callander became famous throughout the world when the Dionne Quintuplets were born. Callander's resident doctor, Allan Roy Dafoe arrived in time to deliver the last two infants and to save the life of the mother. Her babies, all of whom were girls, were named Yvonne, Annette, Cecile, Emilie and Marie.

Suddenly Callander was awash with thousands of tourists. Residents, who had been suffering greatly through the Depression years with the closure of local lumber businesses, began opening up their homes as bed and breakfasts, motels, gift shops and restaurants. In 1939, as the five girls were nearing their fifth birthday the quintuplets, who are wards of the King, were met by the King and Queen in Toronto.

The town was named by a Mr McIntyre, owner of the CC Railway who was given the honour of naming the town that would be developed on a site where the railway construction met the Grand Trunk Railway. However the CCR finally met up with the tracks of the Grand Trunk Railway at South East Bay, beyond the original planned site of the town which McIntyre had already named Callander after his hometown in Scotland. This led to a switch in titles with Callander taking the name of Bonfield and the revised railway meeting point being named Callander.

The name Callander originates from gaelic 'callaidh' meaning 'rapid' or 'caladh' meaning 'hard, stony' and most probably means rapid or hard, stony river, in this case referring to the River Teith which flows through the Scottish town.

The present town of Callander in Ontario has a population of around 3,000 and is a popular retirement spot.

Bannockburn, Illinois was first settled by Irish immigrants in 1835 but named much later after the famous battle site on which Robert the Bruce's army defeated King Edward II of England in 1314. The name derives from the Brittonic words 'bhan' meaning 'bright' and 'oc' or 'ach' meaning 'water'.

Although the state of Illinois was formed in 1818, the population was concentrated in the southern half. The North, where Bannockburn lies remained Indian Territory populated by the Sacs, Foxes, Ottawas, Chippewas and the Potawatomis or 'firemakers'.

During the first thirty years of the nineteenth century these tribes gradually ceded their land to the Government in a series of Treaties which were not always acceptable to the Indians. Chief Black Hawk of the Sacs led his tribe in an attempt to repudiate the pacts. Black Hawk and his men were defeated however, in what became known as the 'Black Hawk War'.

Although the battle never took place in Bannockburn rumour has it, that General Scott, Lieutenant Jefferson Davies and private Abraham Lincoln marched through Lake County on the way to battle. In 1833 the chiefs of the Potawatomis signed a treaty relinquishing the last of their land east of the Mississippi River measuring about five million acres.

The document was signed by seventy four chiefs on consideration that for yielding their land they be given, "A tract of land of like extent as that ceded, five million acres, situated on the east bank of the Missouri River". In addition the government paid $850,000 in cash and goods, $280,000 of which was to be paid in instalments over the following twenty years.

There are still signs of the Indian presence to be found in the area. In Bannockburn there are 'trail trees' and the remains of an Indian council and camp fire area. Telegraph Road, running through the town is an old Indian trail.

The first white settler in Bannockburn was an Irishman named Michael Meehan who had come from County Meath to settle in 1832. The majority of the first settler families were from County Meath, Ireland and the Scottish connection did not appear until almost a century later. Meehan built his home on the Telegraph road, the old Indian trail, naming the site Meehans Settlement, later to be known as Irish Acres. Apart from a short try on the goldfields Meehan lived there until 1876.

The title Bannockburn was chosen by a Scotsman, William

Aitken, who had purchased the land and planned the community using the name Bannockburn. Aitken was a member of the local bridge and golf clubs and in 1924 he suggested the building of homes for the other members. He built the majority of the first homes in Bannockburn. In 1929 an election was held to decide on a name for the community. Of the sixty six votes cast, forty six were in favour of Bannockburn.

Bannockburn Park in Ontario, Canada is situated in Madoc township, just south of Eldorado which was built during a gold rush and is the site of Ontario's first gold mine. Bannockburn began life as a railway terminal. Some residents were employed in the local sawmill and iron mine, and even today the area is still being panned by prospectors in search of gold.

As mentioned Stirling, Alberta was named after J A Stirling, managing director of The Trusts, Executors, and Securities who were based in England and held shares in the Alberta Coal and Railway Company.

The Alberta Coal and Railway Co were given 6400 acres of land for every completed mile of track laid making them the largest land holder in Alberta of that time, with over a million acres. However selling the land was not so easy. Even at \$2.50 per acre, there were not many takers. The British government surveyors had labelled Alberta as the 'arid region' and the 'sterile plains', suitable only for ranching, so the price was lowered to \$1 per acre.

It is hard to believe that Aberfoyle, South Australia is not directly named after the village near Loch Ard, Stirlingshire, Scotland which many Scots regard as the start of the Highlands. In fact the town was named after Christian Sauerbier, who in 1917 was one of many South Australians to change their German sounding names because of ill feeling towards them. Christian chose the name Aberfoyle to replace his surname and then Aberfoyle was named after him. Why he chose this name is unclear but I presume he took the name from the Scottish village.

Arnprior in Ottawa, Canada is named after a priory which was situated on the river Arn in Stirlingshire. Arnprior was named and founded in 1831 when the Buchanan brothers erected a saw and grist mill calling the place after the river in their native Stirlingshire. The entire area was predominately settled by Scots brought over to

Canada by the Highland Chief McNab to form McNab Township. McNab left Scotland in 1822 for Canada and arrived at Arnprior in 1824. He brought with him a party of settlers from the Highlands of Scotland, the first of whom arrived in 1825. Archibald McNab, seventeenth chief of clan McNab, fled Scotland to escape debts inherited from his uncle, the sixteenth chief. Although his forebear had fathered countless children he had no legitimate heir when he died in 1916. Once in Canada McNab tried to re-establish the old feudal system and for a while was successful but finally he had to flee the country once again to escape vengeance from his people in the 1840s. The American town has become known as the town of two beautiful rivers and is located in the County of Renfrew.

Kilsyth, West Virginia has a current population of around 400 residents with no real industry. It is situated in Raleigh County and was named by a Scot, William McKell who operated a colliery on the West Virginian site, naming it after his native Scots town.

Kilsyth, formerly spelt Kilsythe, was incorporated in 1903 and is one of the few towns to be incorporated under what was known as the 'One Man Rule', or whoever ran the coal company. The small town and surrounding area became a major coal mining region.

Other towns bearing Stirlingshire names include three Alvas in the United States, in Kentucky, Oklahoma and Wyoming, a Bannockburn in Ontario and a Bannock County in Idaho.

There is also a Dunblane in Saskatchewan and a Tenterfield in New South Wales, Australia.

There are Stirlings in New Zealand, in Ontario and also in the Northern Territories of Australia where there is also a Stirling Creek. There is a Stirling West in South Australia. Western Australia has a Stirling Range, mountains which run parallel with the south east coast for forty miles rising to 3640 feet.

Australia's Stirling Island is one of the group making up the Solomon Islands, a 900 mile chain of volcanic islands 1,500 miles north of Sydney.

Gazetteer

Abercrombie Scotland Fife. Lat56.12N Long2.47W Small hamlet 1 mile north west of St Monans.

Abercrombie Caves Australia New South Wales. Limestone caves 50 miles south of Bathurst.

Aberdeen Scotland Aberdeenshire. Lat57.08N Long2.07W *pop.* 189,707 (1991) Scotland's third city in size and importance which is situated on the north east coast. The seaport and holiday resort was the site of Scotland's first university. Has been nicknamed the 'Granite City' due to one of the city's industries – granite quarrying. Many buildings in the city are made from this stone. Other industries included fishing and shipbuilding and in the 1960/70s oil discoveries in the North Sea transformed the city into the 'Offshore Capital of Europe'.

Aberdeen Australia Queensland.

Aberdeen Australia New South Wales. Lat32.09 S Long150.53 E *pop.* 1,072 (1961) Town in New South Wales lies 70 miles north west of the coalmining centre of Newcastle. The main industry is coalmining.

Aberdeen Australia Tasmania. District in the City of Devonport on the Mersey River. The first settlers in the area were Scottish and there are several possibilities as to why the town was named Aberdeen.

Aberdeen Canada Saskatchewan. *pop.* 251 (1961) 22 miles north east of Saskatoon, this town was not named after Aberdeen, Scotland but in honour of John Campbell Gordon, the 7th Earl of Aberdeen.

Aberdeen Hong Kong. Lat22.13N Long114.09E A fishing village in the south west of Hong Kong island, on Aberdeen Harbour, 2.5 miles south of Victoria. Main industry is in the shipyards. The Chinese name for the village is Shekpaiwan.

Aberdeen South Africa Cape Province. *pop.* 4,411 (1946) Town in the south east of central Cape Province, on the

Great Karoo. The town was named after the birthplace in Scotland of the Reverend Andrew Murray who became minister of a church built on a nearby farm.

Aberdeen USA Arkansas.

Aberdeen USA California. Lat36.59N Long118.12W.

Aberdeen USA Idaho. Lat42.57N Long112.50W *pop.* 1,468 (1950) Village in Bingham county in the south east of Idaho.

Aberdeen USA Kentucky.

Aberdeen USA Maryland. Lat39.31N Long76.10W. Residential area near Aberdeen Proving Ground (US Army ordnance test centre) and Army chemical centre. Now the largest municipality in Harford County with a population now of 13,087 (1990). On March 22nd, 1892 Aberdeen was incorporated. Economy of the town is boosted by tourism as Aberdeen provides 60% of Harford County's hotels.

Aberdeen USA Mississippi. Lat33.49N Long88.34W. *pop.* 6,837 (1990) County seat of Monroe County, Mississippi. Aberdeen is located on the Tennessee-Tombigbee Waterway in Northeast Mississippi. It was chartered in 1832. It became the county seat in 1849. The modern day industry of Aberdeen ranges from chemicals to plastics, mufflers to bentonite clay.

Aberdeen USA Missouri.

Aberdeen USA New Jersey. Settled in the seventeenth century by Scots Presbyterians who christened their settlement after Aberdeen, Scotland. However the name was not officially recognised until 1977 following a two year campaign by residents.

Aberdeen USA North Carolina. Lat35.08 N Long 79.26 W *pop.* 1,603 (1950) Town in Moore county, North Carolina was incorporated in 1893. It is a trade centre; shipping point for tobacco, fruit and truck area.

Aberdeen USA Ohio. Lat38.40 N Long83.45 W *pop.* 551 (1950) Village in Brown county, in the south west of Ohio. Lies on the Ohio River opposite Maysville, Kentucky.

Aberdeen USA Pennsylvania. Very small community and although listed with operator but no post office or police station.

Aberdeen USA South Dakota. Lat45.28N Long98.30W *pop.* c.25,000 (1995) City is county seat of Brown county, South Dakota. It was settled in 1880, incorporated in 1882. It is a rail and wholesale distribution centre. Other industries include farm machinery, dairy produce flour, wheat, barley, oats and corn.

Aberdeen USA Washington. Lat46.58N Long123.49W *pop.* 16,565 (1990) Port City in Grays Harbour county, Washington. Lies at confluence of Chehalis and Wishkah rivers. It was settled in around 1865 and then incorporated in 1890. Aberdeen is a fishing and lumbering centre.

Aberdeen Bascom USA Indiana. Lat38.54N Long84.59W

Aberdeen Channel Hong Kong. Lat22.14N Long114.10E

Aberdeen Island Hong Kong. Lat22.14N Long114.09E

Aberfoyle Scotland. Lat56.10N Long4.23W Population of village was 719 (1991) The tourist centre of the Trossachs which is surrounded by the Queen Elizabeth Forest Park. The community was mentioned in Walter Scott's *Rob Roy* where the hero met Bailie Nicol Jarvie.

Aberfoyle Australia South Australia. Named after Christian Sauerbier, one of the many South Australians to change their German sounding names because of ill-feeling during World War I. He chose the Scottish name as his surname.

Aberfoyle Park Australia Queensland.

Abernethy Scotland Perthshire.

Lat56.20N Long3.18W *pop.* 895 (1991) It was at Abernethy in 1072 that Malcolm III 'Canmore' met William the Conqueror and they signed the treaty of Abernethy in which Malcolm III acknowledged William as overlord. Malcolm did not have much choice in signing as his 12 year old son was held hostage by the English. Abernethy is also home to an eleventh century round tower, the only other similar tower being in Brechin.

Abernethy Canada Saskatchewan. *pop.* 290 (1948) Village in south east of Saskatchewan.

Airdrie Scotland Lanarkshire. Lat55.38N Long3.58W *pop.* 36,998 (1991) Originally a hamlet in Monklands Parish, the town expanded rapidly in the nineteenth century. Although coal and shale mines existed in the town there was an eighteenth century boom in handloom weaving.

Airdrie Canada Alberta. Town in Alberta was laid out in 1893 and was named by William McKenzie, a railroad engineer after the Lanarkshire burgh where he was born.

Ailsa Craig Scotland. Lat55.80N Long5.07W Rocky Islet in the Firth of Clyde 10 miles off the Ayrshire coast. Affectionately nicknamed 'Paddy's Milestone' as it is situated between Scotland and Ireland.

Ailsa Craig Canada Ontario. The Ontario community was named by Scottish residents after the small island south of Arran, Scotland. The town itself was founded as a result of development by the Grand Trunk Railway in1858. It was first called Craig's Station after its Scots founder, David Craig until it was discovered that there was a town of the same name. He then decided to rename the town after the rock that he could see from his bedroom window as a child inScotland.

Alexandria Scotland Dunbartonshire. Lat55.59N Long3.34W *pop.* 14,150 (1991) The largest town in the Vale of Leven, an area which became famous for the development of bleaching, dyeing and calico-printing in the eighteenth and nineteenth centuries. At one time factories lined the Leven River but the industry declined in the twentieth century.

Alexandria USA Virginia.

Alford Scotland Aberdeenshire. Lat57.14N Long2.42W *pop.* 1,394 (1991) Situated 29.5 miles north west of Aberdeen on the Don River. Scene of the battle of Alford in which

James Graham Marquis of Montrose enticed Lieutenant General Baillie into battle by hiding most of his army behind Gallows Hill.

Alford England. *pop.* 2,218 (1951) Urban district in the east of Lincolnshire which is an agricultural market place.

Alford USA Florida. *pop.* 375 (1950) Town in Jackson county in the northwest of Florida.

Alford USA Massachusetts. *pop.* 212 (1950) Town in Berkshire county, western Massachusetts is a summer resort near New York line.

Alva Scotland Clackmannanshire. Lat58.09N Long3.48W *pop.* 5,201 (1991) Alva is the most central of the Hillfoots villages, situated between Tillicoultry and Menstrie. The village grew substantially in the nineteenth century due to its water powered woollen mills.

Alva USA Kentucky. *pop.*1,341 (1950) The mining village in Harlon county in the south east of Kentucky lies in the Cumberlands, 19 miles east north east of Middlesboro. The main industry is in the bitumous coal mines.

Alva USA Oklahoma. *pop.* 5,495 (1990) Alva was a land office town which played an important role in the opening of the Cherokee Strip. It is now a centre for wheat farming and cattle ranching. City is seat of Woods County in north west Oklahoma. Settled in1863. Lies on salt fork of Arkansas River. Processing centre for agricultural area (especially wheat).

Alva USA Wyoming.

Alva USA Florida. This town was not named after the Scottish Alva but after a native flower of Denmark by a Danish seaman who settled here in the 1880s.

Annan Scotland Dumfriesshire. Lat54.59N Long3.16W *pop.* 8,930 (1991) Royal burgh since at least James V, a port, market town and for some time a centre for handloom weaving. The town has been associated with Robert the Bruce who is said to have resided here before moving to Lochmaben. The Brus Stone, which bears an inscription referring to Robert I was removed from Annan in the nineteenth century and later rediscovered in Devon and returned in1925. Scene of the Battle of Annan.

Annan China. The town has now changed its name to Tsinglung

Annan Canada Ontario.

Annandale Canada Nova Scotia. Annandale, on Prince Edward Island, was named in 1868 by James Johnston, a settler

who emigrated to Canada from Annandale, Scotland in 1840.

Annandale USA New York. *pop.* c.150. Also known as Annandale-on-Hudson, small village in rural Red Hook township. Situated on the east bank of the Hudson River in Dutches County.

Annandale USA Minnesota. Situated in south central Minnesota in Wright County near Clearwater Lake.

Annandale USA New Jersey. Farming area in Hunterdon County.

Annandale USA N Virginia. *pop.* 50,975. Situated in Fairfax County. A large unincorporated community which is largely a residential suburb of Washington DC.

Ardbeg Scotland. There are three Ardbegs in Scotland. One is a village and headland between Rothesay Bay and Kames Bay on the Isle of Bute in the Firth of Clyde; another is in Argyll; the third is a village on Islay 3 miles east of Port Ellen where there is a distillery.

Ardbeg Canada Ontario.

Ardrossan Scotland Ayrshire. Lat55.39N Long4.48W *pop.* 10,750 (1991) Seaport and former resort on the Clyde coast between Irvine and Greenock. Commercial ferry point between Scotland and Ireland. Until 1805 the community consisted of just a handful of houses, however Hugh Montgomerie, 12th Earl of Eglinton planned the town as a seaport connected to Glasgow by canal. Much of the port's trade came from the Eglinton family coal mines but his plans never really took off.

Ardrossan Australia South Australia. *pop.* 558 (1948). A village and sea port on the east coast of Yorke Peninsula in South Australia which was named by Sir James Fergusson, governor of South Australia. Industries are in wheat, wool and limestone.

Argyll Scotland. Former county of Argyllshire is now the local government area of Argyll & Bute. Extensive and spectacularly scenic land area of west Scotland.

Argyle USA Illinois.

Argyll County Australia New South Wales.

Armadale Scotland Isle of Skye

Armadale Scotland West Lothian. Lat55.54N Long3.42W *pop.* 8,958 (1991) Former coal mining town in central Scotland between Glasgow and Edinburgh.

Armadale Australia Western Australia. *pop.* 1,046 (1947) Town in the south west of Western Australia. It is a residential area 17 miles south east of Perth. Named by the South West Railway

Company in 1893.

Armidale Australia New South Wales. *pop.* c.20,000 (1993) Municipality lying in the east of New South Wales. Gold mining centre. Named by a carpenter who was employed in the construction of the railway house. University town and centre of New England region 566 km north of Sydney.

Arn, River Scotland Stirlingshire.

Arnprior, Scotland Stirlingshire Lat56.07N Long4.14W Village and estate 2.25 miles west of Kippen.

Arnprior Canada Ontario. Founded 1831. Named after a priory which was situated on the River Arn, Stirlingshire, Scotland.

Arran Scotland *pop.* c.3,500 (1995) Large island in the Firth of Clyde measuring 20 miles long and 10 miles wide. The population of 3,500 trebles during the summer months. Arran is linked to the mainland by ferry at Ardrossan and Kintyre. The island is split by the Highland boundary fault which means that the northern half of the island is mountainous, some of which can be seen from Islay and Jura, and from tall buildings in Glasgow. The southern half has a gentler landscape.

Arran Canada Saskatchewan.

Arran Canada Ontario.

Arrochar Scotland
Dunbartonshire. Lat56.12N
Long4.45W Village with pier
at the head of Loch Long

Arrochar USA New York. A
section of Richmond
Borough in New York City on
east Statten Island.

Ayr Scotland Ayrshire. Lat55.28N
Long4.27W *pop.* 47,692
(1991) Resort town situated
on Ayr River. Its history dates
back to the early thirteenth
century when it was granted
a charter by William the Lion.
In 1297 Ayr was the scene of
one of William Wallace's first
confrontations with the
English. In 1315 the first
meeting of a Scottish
Parliament was held after the
victory at Bannockburn. Ayr
has also been closely
associated with Robert Burns
whose birthplace, Alloway is
now a suburb of the town.
Today Ayr is home to the
Scottish Grand National.

Ayr USA Nebraska. *pop.* 121
(1950) Village in Adams
county in the south of
Nebraska. It lies 10 miles
south of Hastings on Little
Blue River.

Ayr USA North Dakota. *pop.* 104
(1950) Village in Cass county
in the east of North Dakota. It
lies 16 miles north west of
Casselton.

Ayr Australia Queensland. The
town in Queensland was
surveyed and gazetted in

1881 and the following year
named after Ayr, Scotland,
the birthplace of the then
State Premier, Sir Thomas
McIllwraith (1835-1900).
Small town south of
Townsville. The area is noted
for its beautiful beaches.

Ayr Canada Ontario. The
community of Ayr in Ontario
was also named after this
town by Scottish settlers, one
of whom was James
Jackson, who named the Nith
River in this Province.

Ayre Scotland Orkney. Lat59.09N
Long2.37W

Ayr, Mount USA Iowa. Ringgold
County. The Iowa town is
named after the Scottish
town of Ayr with the first
word of the name refering to
the high location of the place
between the Missouri and
Mississippi Rivers at this
point. The town was named
by a visitor who thought that
Ayr was one of the prettiest
names on the Scottish map.

Ayrshire USA Iowa. *pop.* 334
(1950) Town in Palo Alto
county in the north west of
Iowa. Livestock and grain
area. Ayrshire was founded
when the Des Moines and
Fort Dodge railroads were
built through the area. The
town had a number of names
before being called Ayrshire,
supposedly after a Scotsman
who said the area reminded
him of his home.

Bal Clutha New Zealand South Island. The town of Bal Clutha in Otago, South Island, was originally known as Clutha Ferry taking its name from the Clutha River on which it stands. The river was given its title by Scottish settlers from an early Celtic name of the River Clyde in Scotland. The 'Bal' part of the name is common in many Scottish placenames, such as Balmoral and Balfour, and means simply village or settlement.

Balmoral Scotland Aberdeenshire. Lat57.03N Long3.13W Famous royal residence situated on the River Dee 10km north of Braemar. The Balmoral Estate was mentioned as far back as the fifteenth century. When Sir Robert Gordon died in 1848 the Queen and Prince Consort took over the lease. Five years later they purchased Balmoral for £31,500. They demolished the Gordon house replacing it with the granite castle in 1855, designed by William Smith of Aberdeen.

Balmoral Canada New Brunswick. Named by Scottish settlers after the famous royal residence in Scotland, Balmoral Castle. As the castle did not become a royal residence until 1852, when it was purchased by Prince Albert, the name may be quite late.

Banff Scotland Banffshire. *pop.* 4,110 (1991) Former county town of Banffshire in NE Scotland which stretched from the Cairngorms to the Moray Firth.

Banff Canada Alberta. *pop.* 5,688 (1990) Originally called siding 29 (a proposed tunnel site). The community of Banff, Alberta is situated in the well known Banff National Park, both named after the Scottish town. The name was suggested by John H MacTavish, Land Commissioner of the Canadian Pacific Railway as the Scottish town was not far from the birthplace of the railway's president from1881-1888, Sir George Stephen (Baron Maint Stephen).

Bannockburn Scotland Stirlingshire. Lat56.05N Long3.55W *pop.* 5,746 (1991) The town which lies near the famous battlefield where Robert the Bruce defeated the English on 24th June 1314. For some time the town was famous for its tartan weaving which was later to be replaced by coal mining.

Bannockburn USA Illinois. *pop.* 249 (1950) Village in Lake county. It lies 25 miles north west of Chicago. Bannockburn was first settled by Irish immigrants in 1835.

Bannockburn Park Canada Ontario. Situated in Madoc Township, just south of Eldorado, a town which was built during the gold rushes. It is the scene of Ontario's first goldmine.

Bannockburn Zimbabwe Lat20.16S Long29.51E

Bannock USA Idaho. *pop.* 41,745 (1950) County in the south east of Idaho. The seat is Pocatello. It was formed in 1893 in the mountain area drained by the Bear and Portneuf Rivers. The irrigated fields produce wheat, alfalfa, sugar beets, livestock dairying. Manufacturing at Pocatello and manganese deposits are the other industries.

Barrhead Scotland Renfrewshire. Lat55.47N Long4.23W *pop.* 16,876 (1991) Small industrial town to the south west of Glasgow which was created by the merger of several small villages on the banks of the Levern Water. These villages had expanded in the eighteenth century because of the growth of the textile industry and the development of bleach and dyeing processes carried out here. Barrhead was home to one of Scotland's first cotton spinning mills in 1780, several small coal mines and to the sanitary engineering firm Shanks.

Barrhead Canada Alberta. *pop.* 4,160 (1990) Situated in Paddle River Valley. An historic fur trading trail is situated here. The town was named in 1913 by directors of a local cooperative after Barrhead Scotland, a manufacturing town where there had been a similar collective force.

Bathgate Scotland West Lothian. Lat55.54N Long3.38W *pop.* 13,819 (1991) The industrial town is believed to have been given by Robert Bruce to his daughter Marjorie on her wedding to Walter the High Steward in 1316. The town was once a staging post on the Edinburgh–Glasgow road. Bathgate expanded rapidly in the eighteenth century as it became a centre of handloom weaving and later of coal and shale mining. In 1850 James 'Paraffin' Young set up his first paraffin refinery in Bathgate.

Bathgate USA North Dakota. *pop.* 209 (1950) City in Pembina county in the north east of North Dakota. It lies10 miles north east of Cavaliar on the Tongue River.

Ben Lomond Scotland. Long56.11N Lat 4.38W Mountain on east side of Loch Lomond. Alt 3192ft.

Ben Lomond National Park Australia Tasmania. The mountain mass in Tasmania was named in 1894 by the explorer and Lieutenant-Governor of New South Wales, William Patterson, after his native Scottish mountain Ben Lomond. Other places of the name also derive directly or indirectly from the same source. Walking and skiing area in the north east of the main island.

Ben Lomond Canada New Brunswick.

Ben Lomond Australia New South Wales. Mountain in New England Range which rises 1,520 ft forming part of the Great Dividing Range.

Ben Lomond New Zealand South Island.

Ben Nevis Scotland Inverness-shire. The highest mountain in the British Isles measuring 1343m(4406ft). Ben Nevis is situated near Fort William. The name Nevis comes from the Gaelic 'neamh' which means 'heaven' or 'clouds' therefore the name refers to 'the mountain with its head in the clouds'

Ben Nevis New Zealand South Island.

Biggar Scotland Lanarkshire. Lat55.37 N Long3.31W *pop.* 1,994 (1991) Situated between Lanark and Peebles, Biggar was given burgh status in 1451. William Wallace is believed to have defeated a large army of English at the Battle of Biggar.

Biggar Canada Saskatchewan. *pop.* 1,799 (1948) Town in the west of Saskatchewan. The town is a railroad junction, has grain elevators and lumbering. Although name isidentical was not named after Scottish town of Biggar.

Blantyre Scotland Lanarkshire. Lat55.48N Long4.06W *pop.* 18,484 (1991) The vestiges of a priory built in Blantyre in the thirteenth century still stand beside the Clyde opposite the castle. David Dale, famous for establishing New Lanark cotton mills also created a mill at Bothwell. The town was also the scene of an horrific mining explosion in which 207 men lost their lives. The explosion occurred on 22nd October, 1877, thought to have been the result of a naked flame or shot firing. Another 28 men died in a further accident two years later.

Blantyre Malawi. The largest city in Malawi, founded in 1876 as a Church of Scotland mission station and was named after the Scottish birthplace of David Livingstone (see Livingstone), the town of Blantyre, Lanarkshire.

Bothwell Scotland Lanarkshire. Lat55.48N Long4.04W *pop.* 6,542 (1991)

Bothwell Canada Ontario. Named in about 1856 by

George Brown, of the *Toronto Globe* newspaper, after the Scottish town of Bothwell in Lanarkshire from which his family had originated.

Bothwell Australia Tasmania. Small town near Hobart. Church dates back to 1857.

Braemar Scotland Aberdeenshire. Lat57.00N Long3.25W Situated on the River Dee, the town is a popular tourist centre in Royal Deeside. Braemar Castle replaced an earlier Kindrochit Castle which was destroyed by 1620.

Braemar Australia South Australia.

Brechin Scotland Angus. *pop.* 7,655 (1991) Although Brechin is a small town it does have a genuine claim to be a city. It was once a Bishopric and has a Cathedral. The present Cathedral which stands above the South Esk dates back to the thirteenth century. Its football team is called Brechin City.

Brechin Canada Ontario.

Burnside New Zealand. Area in the City of Dunedin boundary, South Island.

Cairns Australia Queensland. *pop.* 39,000 (1976) May be named after Cairngorms, Cairn River or a number of other places in Scotland with a similar name. Tourist centre and excursion starting point for the Great Barrier Reef. An impressive city from the air when the plane descends low over the mountains covered with tropical rain forest. Large deep natural harbour.

Caledonia County USA Vermont. The ancient Roman name of Scotland is found adopted in a few United States towns and counties, such as Caledonia County, Vermont.

Caledonia USA Minnesota.

Caledonia Canada Nova Scotia. Situated on the south coast of Prince Edward Island.

Calgary Canada Alberta. *pop.* 710,677 (1990) The city in southern Alberta was originally called Fort Brisebois when it was established in 1875 as a post of the North West Mounted Police. The following year it was renamed Fort Calgary by Colonel James F Macleod of the Royal Canadian Mounted Police after the Scottish village of Calgary on the Isle of Mull, where some of his ancestors and family lived.

Calgary Bay Scotland Isle of Mull. Situated 13 miles south west of Tobermory.

California Scotland Stirlingshire.

Callander Scotland Perthshire. Lat56.14N Long4.12W *pop.* 2,622 (1991) One of the many communities in Scotland nicknamed 'The Gateway to the Highlands', the town owes its existence to the Commissioners for Forfeited (Jacobite) Estates who selected this section of the forfeited Drummond land for development in the eighteenth century. The town became popular in the nineteenth century due to the Victorian spas.

Callander Canada Ontario. The Ontario village was named after the Scottish town of Callander in Perthshire where the first postmaster of the village, George Morrison, was born. The town became renowned in the 1930s when quintuplets were born here.

Campbellton Scotland Dumfries & Galloway Lat54.51N Long4.06W

Campbellton Canada New Brunswick. Settled in 1750s by Acadians and then by Scots in the 1820s when the area became a centre for fishing and shipbuilding. It is situated at the head of ocean navigation on the Restigouche River.

Campbelltown Scotland Argyll. Lat55.25N Long5.37W *pop.* 5,722 (1991) A royal burgh situated at the top of Loch Campbelltown. The town was originally founded as Kinlochkilkerran in 1607 by the 7th Earl of Argyll as part of a plantation policy. Between 1817 and 1880 a total of 34

whisky distilleries were established but in the1920s many of these closed and several amalgamated leaving only two which survive today. The other major industry of the town was herring fishing which also declined.

Campbelltown Australia.

Carberry Scotland East Lothian. Lat56.00N Long3.09W

Carberry Canada Manitoba. The community in Manitoba was named in 1882 after Carberry tower near Musselburgh, the Scottish home of the then Lord Elphinstone, who was a director of the Canadian Pacific Railway.

Cardross Scotland Dunbartonshire. *pop.* 1,958 (1991) Situated on the River Clyde between Dumbarton and Helensburgh. Robert I died in Cardross Castle in 1329 after which his heart was encased and is believed to have been buried at Melrose Abbey following an abortive attempt to take it to the Holy Land.

Cardross Canada Saskatchewan.

Carrick Scotland Ayrshire. Ayrshire was split into three ancient regalities, Kyle, Carrick and Cunningham. Measuring 32 miles long and 20 miles wide Carrick consists mainly of remote glens and hills. Once the home of the Bruce family who acquired the Earldom of

Carrick in 1297 when Robert de Bruce married Marjorie, Countess of Carrick. Their son became Robert I.

Carrick Canada Ontario.

Carrick USA Pennsylvania. Carrick is a residential neighbourhood on the south side of Pittsburg, Pennsylvania on the slope of Mount Washington.

Cathkin Braes Scotland. Hill ridge near Glasgow, 2 miles east of Carmunnock. Alt 629ft.

Cathkin Peak South Africa. Cathkin Peak, a mountain in the Drakensberg range near Champagne Castle, was named after Cathkin Braes, by a David Gray, a Scot who settled in Natal in 1849. The mountain was itself named Champagne Castle at one time, until the name was transferred to the neighbouring peak. David Gray was behind the naming of Champagne Castle too, allegedly referring to a fight he had with a climbing partner over a bottle of champagne.

Cessnock Castle Scotland Ayrshire. Lat55.35N Long4.21W Situated near the village of Galston.

Cessnock Australia New South Wales. The city, now part of Greater Cessnock in New South Wales, arose as a coal mining town in the 1880s. The town is believed to have

been named by the original land grantee, James Campbell. The Scotsman is said to have been inspired by Robert Burns poem *On Cessnock Banks*. However, the actual origin could have been Cessnock Castle in Scotland which was named after the burn in this poem.

Clutha River New Zealand. The river was given the early Celtic name of the River Clyde in Scotland. It is New Zealand's largest river on which stands the community of Bal Clutha. (See Bal Clutha.)

Clyde, River Scotland. The Scottish river was once one of the chief commercial waterways in the world with some of world's greatest shipbuilding firms on the river between Glasgow and Greenock. Shipbuilding declined following the Second World War. Scotland's third longest river after Tay and Spey.

Clyde Canada North West Territories. The Clyde on Baffin Island, North West Territories, located on Clyde Inlet, was named in 1818 by the Arctic explorer John Ross, uncle of James Ross, as a compliment to the Scottish river.

Clyde River Canada Ontario.

Clyde River USA New York. It is likely that the Clyde River,

New York, was named after its Scottish counterpart.

Clyde USA Ohio. *pop.* 5,776 (1990) City in Sandusky County, in northern Ohio on Raccoon Creek. The city was settled in the 1820s and is now an agricultural trade and service centre for surrounding area. Sherwood Anderson lived here between 1884-96 and is thought to have modeled Winesburgh on the town.

Colonsay Scotland Inner Hebrides. Lat56.04N Long6.13W *pop.* c.90 (1994) This tiny island which measures just eight miles long and three miles wide at its widest point lies NE-SW. In 1841 Colonsay and its neighbour Oronsay had a population of almost 1,000, but this has declined to under 100.

Colonsay Canada Saskatchewan. Town born due to the construction of the Canadian Pacific Railway. Not only has the town been named after the Scottish island but the street names have been taken from the Hebrides too.

Corstorphine New Zealand. As a result of local government reorganisation is now situated within the new City of Dunedin boundary, covering 3,350squ km. Named after the residential district of Edinburgh,

Scotland. Dunedin itself was named after the Gaelic name for Edinburgh.

Culloden Scotland Inverness-shire. Lat57.29N Long4.07W *pop.* 3,669 (1991). Famous battlefield near Inverness, the scene of the last pitched battle on British soil when Highlanders under Prince Charles Edward Stuart were defeated by the Royal troops under the command of Duke of Cumberland on 16th April 1746.

Culloden Canada. Situated on the south coast of Prince Edward Island.

Cupar Scotland Fife. Lat56.19N Long3.01N *pop.* 7,545 (1991) Cupar was the county town of Fife and the ancient seat of the MacDuff Earls of Fife. It was granted a charter to become a royal burgh in the fourteenth century.

Cupar Canada Saskatchewan. *pop.* 369 (1948 Lies 40 miles northeast of Regina. The main industries are grain elevators and flourmills.

Currie Scotland Midlothian. Lat55.54N Long3.18N Village which is situated on the Water of Leith, 6 miles south west of Edinburgh.

Currie Australia Tasmania. *pop.* 513 (1950) The town and port on King Island is positioned on the Bass Strait. This is the largest town and port of King Island. It is a sheep centre.

Currie USA Minnesota. *pop.* 551
(1950) The village in Murray
county in the south west of
Minnesota. It is a grain,
livestock and poultry area. It
is positioned on the Des
Moines River 7 miles north
east of Slayton.

Currie USA North Carolina. The
village in Pender county in
the south east of North
Carolina was established in
1926 as a military park. There
is a commemoratory battle of
Mooers Creek Bridge (Feb.
1776).

Dallas Scotland Morayshire.
Village in the centre of Moray
beside River Lossie. Acquired
by landowner William de
Ripley from the Crown in
1279. A knighthood went with
it and he became known as
Sir William of Dallas.

Dallas USA Texas. *pop.* Dallas –
Fort Worth Metropolis
2.5million (1971) Founded as
a trading post in 1844 and
developed as a focus of the
cotton trade, then as a
mineral and oil producing
centre, and later as a bank
and insurance operations
centre. Got its name in 1845
from a politician, George
Mifflin Dallas, a descendant
of William of Dallas. George
Dallas had become vice-
president of the US the
previous year.

Darvel Scotland Ayrshire.
Lat55.37N Long4.18W Small

village and parish 9 miles
east of Kilmarnock. A major ·
lace making centre, which
despite a decline in the
industry is still carried out
here in the traditional
manner.

Darvel Bay Malaysia. Might be
named after Darvel, Scotland.

Deloraine Burn Scotland Borders
Lat55.28N Long3.02W By the
river Ettrick, 13 miles
southwest of Selkirk.

Deloraine Australia Tasmania.
The town of Deloraine,
Tasmania takes its name
from either William of
Deloraine, a fictional knight
in Scott's *The Lady Of The
Lost Minstrel*, or directly from
the place (or burn) of this
name (which Scott used for
the knight), near Selkirk,
Scotland. The former is
possible as the town surveyor
was related to Scott and the
name could thus have been
an imaginative tribute to him.
The Tasmanian town was
founded in the late 1840s.

Denny Scotland Stirlingshire.
Lat56.01N Long3.55W *pop.*
11,061 (1991) Town and
parish 12 miles south of
Stirling.

Denny USA

Dingwall Scotland Ross &
Cromarty. Lat57.58N
Long4.25W *pop.* 5,228 (1991)
On the river Peffer where it
enters the Cromarty Firth.
Macbeth is said to have been

born in Dingwall. The name is believed to have derived from the Norse 'Thing Vollr' which means 'the field of the thing' which refers to the Parliament. Nothing remains of the castle which is credited to William the Lion. The once important harbour has also disappeared.

Dingwall Canada Nova Scotia. *pop.* c.150 (1950) The village in Nova Scotia lies on Aspy Bay on the north of Cape Breton Island. Industries include gypsum, quarrying and fishing.

Don, River Scotland. Rises near Bannfshire borders and flows east to the North Sea, 1 mile north east of Old Aberdeen. The Don is one of the best fishing rivers in Scotland.

Douglas Scotland Lanarkshire. Lat55.33 Long3.51W *pop.* 1,616 (1991) This land is thought to have been granted to either a William or Theobald Fleming in the thirteenth century whose descendants changed their name to Douglas, adopting it for their castle and subsequent township. Their family became one of the most powerful in Scotland.

Douglas Brazil. Village in Northern District. Lies in Honduras on Hondo River.

Douglas Canada Ontario. *pop.* c.500 (1950) In south east Ontario on Bonnechere River.

Douglas England Isle of Man. County seat of Isle of Man

Douglas Ireland County Cork. Lies in south east central County Cork.

Douglas South Africa Cape province. Lies in north east of Cape Province on Vaal River seven miles east of its mouth on Orange River. Town changed hands several times during South African War.

Douglas USA Alaska. Town in east Alaska on East Douglas Island, in Alexander Archipelago, on Gastineau Channel. The town was a residential section for Juneau gold miners and grew up after 1881 during operation of the treadwell mines.

Douglas USA Arizona. *pop.* 12,822. City in Cochise County in the extreme south east of Arizona which is a ranching and copper mining trade centre.

Douglas USA Arkansas

Douglas USA Colorado. *pop.* 3,507 (1950) County in central Colorado whose seat is Castle Rock. Formed in 1861. Covers 843 squ miles.

Douglas USA Georgia. *pop.* 10,464. Situated in Coffee County. The city contains one of the State's major tobacco markets.

Douglas USA Massachusetts.

Douglas USA Michegan.

Douglas USA Nebraska.

Douglas USA North Dakota.

Douglas USA Oklahoma.

Douglas USA Wyoming.

Douglas, Cape USA Alaska.

Douglas, Fort USA Utah. Salt Lake
City.

Douglas County USA Georgia.
County in north west central
Georgia whose seat is
Douglasville.

Douglas County USA Illinois.

Douglas County USA Kansas.

Douglas County USA Minnesota.

Douglas County USA Montana.

Douglas County USA Nebraska.

Douglas County USA Nevada.

Douglas County USA Oregon.

Douglas County USA South
Dakota.

Douglas County USA Washington.

Douglas County USA Wisconsin.

Douglas Dam USA Tennessee. In
French Broad River. Major
TVA dam for flood control
and power. 202ft high, 1,705ft
wide. Completed in 1943.

Douglas Island USA Alaska. Site
of famous Treadwell Mine.

Douglas Lake USA Michigan.
Lake in Cheboygan county
north Michigan. University of
Michigan Biological Station is
here.

Douglas USA Kansas. City in
Butler county on Walnut
River.

Douglas Station Canada
Manitoba. 12 miles ENE of
Brandon.

Douglaston USA New York. A
residential section of Queens
borough in New York City.

Douglastown Canada New

Brunswick. Village in north
east of state on Miramichi
River 3 miles west of
Chatham.

Douglasville USA Georgia. County
seat of Douglas county.

Dumfries Scotland Dumfries-
shire. Lat55.04N Long3.36W
pop. 32,136 (1991) In the
extreme south of Scotland
near the border with England.
Also referred to as the
'Queen of the South' which is
the name used by the local
football team. The town was
prosperous in the nineteenth
century with the busiest port
in southern Scotland. The
castle and town changed
hands several times during
the Wars of Independence
and the Border disturbances.

Dumfries Canada Ontario. Town
named by William Dickson
(1769-1846), born in
Dumfries, Scotland. He
emigrated to Canada in 1792
and practised as a lawyer. In
1816 he bought 100,000 acres
and by 1817 there were 38
families settled, mainly Scots
who had previously lived in
Genesee County, New York.

Dumfries USA Virginia Lat38.34N
Long77.21W *pop.* c.5,000
(1994) The town in Virginia
lies just east of Prince
William Forest Park. The
town was settled by wealthy
tobacco merchants and
around 3,500 Jacobite
prisoners following their

defeat at Culloden in 1746.

Dunbar Scotland East Lothian. Lat55.60N Long2.31W *pop.* 6,518 (1991) Became a royal burgh in 1445 and home to the earls of Dunbar until their forfeiture to James I in 1434. Two battles were fought at Dunbar, the first in 1296 when Edward I demanded that John Balliol supply Scots troops to fight France but he refused. Edward I invaded Scotland, first taking Berwick then Dunbar four weeks later. The port town has been an important fishing town for centuries. During the eighteenth century Dunbar was one of Scotland's major herring ports. Dunbar now a popular holiday resort claiming to be the driest and sunniest spot in Scotland.

Dunbar Australia Queensland.

Dunbar USA Nebraska. *pop.* 228 (1950) Village in Otoe county in the south east of Nebraska. It lies 8 miles west of Nebraska city on a branch of Little Nemaha River.

Dunbar USA Oklahoma.

Dunbar USA Pennsylvania. *pop.* 1,363 (1950) The borough in Fayette county in south west Pennsylvania lies between Connellsville and Union town.

Dunbar USA Utah.

Dunbar USA West Virginia. *pop.* 8,967 (1990) The industrial city in Kanawha county, western West Virginia was incorporated in 1921. It lies in a coal mining region on the Kanawha River. Other industries include oil wells, manufacturing of farm implements, glass products and enamelware.

Dunbar USA Wisconsin.

Dunbar Heights Canada British Columbia. Residential suburb of Vancouver.

Dumbarton Scotland Dunbartonshire. Lat55.57N Long2.31W *pop.* 21,962 (1991) Dumbarton Rock, a 240ft rock of basalt which towers over the town was originally known as 'Dun Breatann' which meant 'Fortress ofthe Britons' was fortified since at least the fifth century. A royal burgh since 1222 it rivalled both Glasgow and Rutherglen as a market town in the fifteenth century becoming the county town of Dunbartonshire. The town was also made famous by shipbuilding which started in the eighteenth century. By 1853 there were five shipyards including William Denny who engineered the *Cutty Sark*. William Denny ceased production in the 1960s. Now whisky distilling and warehousing have replaced shipbuilding.

Dunbarton USA New Hampshire. *pop.* 1700 (1995) The town in Merrimade county, in south central New Hampshire is 9 miles south west of Concord. The town was settled by the Stark family who had emigrated from Dumbarton Scotland.

Dunbarton USA South Carolina. *pop.* 262 (1950) Nobody lives in Dunbarton today. The former town in Barnwell county, South Carolina lies 25 miles south east of Aiken, in an area taken over by US Atomic Energy Commission for its Savannah River plant which works with hydrogen bomb materials.

Dunblane Scotland Perthshire. Lat56.11N Long3.58W *pop.* 7,621 (1991) The town was named after St Blane from Bute who is believed to have established a church around the turn of the seventh century by the Water of Allan. The town still has a cathedral and became a spa in Victorian times.

Dunblane Canada Saskatchewan.

Dundee Scotland Lat56.29N Long3.02W *pop.* 158,981 (1991) Situated on the north shore of the Firth of Tay the city was the site of a Mesolithic settlement which later grew to form modern Dundee. On top of Dundee Law, a 182m hill there was once an Iron Age fort called 'Dun Diagh' from which the town probably received its name. The first reference to a more substantial settlement was in 1054, and by the twelfth century was a well established town. Granted a royal charter in 1190, the town was later given status of Sheriffdom in 1359 sending representatives to Parliament. From1690 the town had a prominent linen manufacturing industry. Jute later replaced flax by 1855 as main fibre.

Dundee Australia New South Wales. Lat29.34 S 151.30 E

Dundee Canada Quebec. Settled by early Scots settlers who were mainly from the Highlands.

Dundee South Africa. Natal. Lat28.10S Long30.15E The town in Natal near Glencoe was laid out in 1882 and named after the Scottish city, the birthplace of its founder, Thomas Paterson Smith. The town is situated near four battlefields of the Anglo–Zulu war and has become a tourist attraction.

Dundee USA Florida. Lat27.59N Long81.37W *pop.* 1,152 (1950). Town in Polk county in central Florida. The industry includes packing citrus fruit.

Dundee USA Illinois Lat42.06N Long88.18W The village in Kane County, Illinois lies just north of Elgin, which was named after Elgin, Scotland.

It is composed of East and West Dundee, on either side of the Fox River. It lies in an agricultural area.

Dundee USA Indiana. Lat40.16N Long85.44W

Dundee USA Iowa. Lat42.35N Long91.33W *pop.* 176 (1950) Town in Delaware county in the east of Iowa. It lies on the Maquoketa River. Its main industry is a fish hatchery.

Dundee USA Kansas.

Dundee USA Michigan Lat41.58N Long83.38W *pop.* c.2,600 (1995) The village in Monroe county in the extreme south east of Michigan was settled in 1827 and incorporated in 1855. It is positioned on the Raisin River and lies in an agricultural area. Dundee was settled in 1823 and originally called Winfield but was renamed in 1836 by Alonzo Curtis, the first postmaster after his hometown in Scotland. One of the industries ofthe town is a cement factory which is called Dundee Cement. It is near an Indian Reservation.

Dundee USA Minnesota. *pop.* 179 (1950) Situated in Nobles County. Village lies in grain and potato area.

Dundee USA Mississippi. Lat34.30N Long90.30W *pop.* c.60 (1995) Town was first known as Carnsville after a Captain Carnsville when it was settled in 1884 but in 1887 when the town was incorporated the Post Office objected to the name and changed it to Dundee. They claimed the name was too similar to other towns. Dundee is currently a very small unincorporated village.

Dundee USA Missouri.

Dundee USA New York. Lat42.32N Long76.59W *pop.* 1,165 (1950) Village in Yates county, New York, incorporated 1847. It lies in Finger Lakes grape growing region and is a summer resort.

Dundee USA Oregon. Lat45.18N Long123.02W *pop.* 308 (1950) The city is in Yamhill county in the north west of Oregon. The main industries are walnuts, filberts and prunes. Named by William Reid who arrived in Oregon in 1874 from Dundee, Scotland.

Dundee USA Texas Lat33.45N Long98.55W *pop.* c.300 (1950) The village in Archer county in the north of Texas, 25 miles WSW of Wichita Falls has a State fish hatchery on the Wichita River nearby.

Dundee USA Wisconsin. Lat43.39 N Long88.11 W

Dundee Bight Canada. Lat76.00N Long99.45W

Dundee Island Antarctica. Lat63.30S Long56.00W Nobody lives on this island which was discovered in 1893 by the Scottish explorer,

Thomas Robertson. It is 15
nautical miles long, 10
nautical miles wide. It lies off
the east tip of Palmer
Peninsula, south west of
Joinville Island.
Dundee Roll USA Indiana.
Lat40.33N Long85.23W
Dunedin New Zealand South
Island. Lat45.52S
Long170.31E *pop.* c.118,000
(1993) The city on the south
east coast of South Island
was settled in 1848 by
Scottish settlers as a Scottish
Free Church settlement, one
of the early settlers being
William Cargill. It was at first
called New Edinburgh. The
Gaelic name of Edinburgh
(properly known as Din
Eydin, 'fortress of Eydin') was
then substituted as more
original and historic. It lies at
the base of Ottago Peninsula
which forms Ottago Harbour.
Dunedin USA Florida. *pop.* 34,012
(1990) City in Pinellas county,
western Florida. Originally
known as Jonesboro in 1860,
after a local store owner
when it was first settled.
Settled around 1865,
incorporated 1899. The name
changed however when in
1882, two Scotsmen named J
O Douglas and James
Summerville made an official
request for a post office and
proposed the same historic
name of Edinburgh for it. It is
a resort on the Gulf Coast

adjacent to Clearwater. City is
now a winter resort and
fishing centre. Industries
include processing citrus fruit
and manufacture of canning
and packing machinery.
Dunoon Scotland Argyll.
Lat56.57N Long4.55W *pop.*
9,038 (1991) Town on north
shore of Firth of Clyde which
is 21 miles by river from
Glasgow.
Dunoon Australia New South
Wales. District in the city of
Lismore which is mainly a
Greek and Italian community.
Dunkeld Scotland Perthshire.
Lat56.34N Long3.35W *pop.*
1,227 (1991) Much of the
town was burned to the
ground in 1689 when the
Highlanders descended on
the Cameronians who held
Dunkeld. Modern day
Dunkeld comprises two
streets beside the Tay.
Alexander Mackenzie, who
went on to become Prime
Minister of Canada, spent his
childhood in Dunkeld.
Dunkeld Australia Queensland.
This town owes its title to
Major Thomas Mitchell, the
namer of Scone, New South
Wales.
Dunkeld Australia Victoria.
Dunmaglass Scotland Inverness-
shire. Lat57.26N Long4.41W
Estate and shooting lodge 6
miles east of Inverfarigaig
pier on Loch Ness.
Dunmaglass Canada Nova

Scotia. The community in Nova Scotia was founded by Scottish settlers from Dunmaglass, an estate near Foyers, Invernessshire and was named after it.

Dunvegan Scotland Isle of Skye. Lat57.27N Long6.35W Village with inn on Dunvegan Loch. Dunvegan Castle still is the principal seat of MacLeod after being given to Leod, the first chief when he married the daughter of the Norse Seneschal of Skye in the thirteenth century.

Dunvegan Canada Nova Scotia. The community on Cape Breton Island, Nova Scotia was originally known as Broad Cove Marsh. The name was changed in 1885 to Dunvegan as a Scottish link with Dunvegan and especially its castle on the Isle of Skye.

Edenburg South Africa Orange Free State. The town was laid out in 1862 and although some may believe the name is of Biblical origin, referring to a new 'Garden of Eden', it is possible that the name is a version of Edinburgh, which was the native city of the only minister here in the Orange Free State, the Rev Andrew Murray (1828-1917).

Edina USA Minnesota. *pop.* 46,070 (1990) The village in Minnesota derives its name from Edinburgh Scotland, developing around the Edina Flour Mill (itself named Edinburgh). The name marks a Scottish emigrant connection.

Edina USA Missouri. The city in Missouri also derives its name from the Scottish city from an emigrant connection.

Edinboro USA Pennsylvania. Lat41.53 N Long80.08W *pop.* 7,736 (1990) A resort borough in Erie county, in the north west of Pennsylvania. There is a state teachers' college here and the main industry is lumbering. It lies 17 miles south of Erie. The 'burgh' part of the name was changed as the residents had difficulty pronouncing it.

Edinburg Latvia. Resort in Rigas Jurmala (or Rigas Yurmala), which since 1946 has been within Riga city limits. Riga consists of 6 amalgamated resorts linked by electric railroad.

Edinburg USA Illinois. Lat39.40 N Long89.23 W *pop.* 921 (1950) Village in Christian county, central Illinois.

Edinburg USA Indiana. Lat39.21N Long85.59W *pop.* 3,283 (1950) Town on Johnson-Bartholomew county line, Indiana. Settled in 1821 on the east fork of White River. US army camp Atterbury is just west of the community.

Edinburg USA Maine. *pop.* 36 (1950) A town in Penobscot

county in south central
Maine. It lies on the
Penobscot and 14 miles
above Old Town. The main
industry is lumbering.
Edinburg USA Mississippi.
Lat32.49 N Long89.20W
Edinburg USA Missouri.
Lat40.04N Long93.43W
Edinburg USA New Jersey.
Lat40.15N Long74.36W
Edinburg USA New York.
Lat43.10N Long74.10W First
settled in 1787 by the Stark
family many of whom had
seen action in the War of
Independence and had seen
the area while doing so. First
called Northfield until it was
discovered that there was a
town of the same name.
Edinburg USA North Dakota.
Lat48.31N Long97.51W *pop.*
343 (1950) Village in Walsh
county in the north east of
North Dakota. It lies 22 miles
west north west of Grafton.
Named by a Norwegian after
the university where he
studied in Scotland. The town
was completely destroyed by
fire in 1900 but rebuilt the
following year.
Edinburg USA Texas. Lat26.18N
Long98.10W *pop.* 29,885
(1990) The Texan city was
originally founded (on a
nearby site) as Old
Edinburgh, named after the
native city of founder John
Young. In 1908 it was moved
to what was then called

Chapin, a settlement
established the previous year.
It was incorporated as
Chapin in 1908 and was then
renamed in 1911. The city is
the county seat of Hidalgo
County in the extreme south
of Texas, in lower Rio Grande
Valley. The main industries of
the city are the trade, packing
and processing of citrus fruit.
Oil and natural gas wells are
also located nearby.
Edinburg USA Virginia. *pop.* 553
(1950) Town in Shenandoah
county in the north west of
Virginia near the north fork of
Shenandoah River in an
agricultural area. Named
after Garden of Eden – not
named after Edinburgh,
Scotland
Edinburgh Scotland Midlothian.
Lat55.57N Long3.10W *pop.*
401,910 (1991) The capital of
Scotland grew up around its
castle on an extinct volcano.
It is referred to as Dun Edin
as far back as the sixth
century. It was made a royal
burgh in the twelfth century
after David I founded
Holyrood Abbey in 1128 and
grew up around the castle
rock. Was the seat of Scottish
Parliament before the Act of
Union with England in 1707.
Edinburgh was a major
intellectual centre during the
eighteenth century and is
now a major university town
and a centre of insurance,

finance and electronics. More than 1.2million tourists visit Edinburgh castle every year. The city is host to the world famous annual International Festival of the Arts.

Edinburgh Tristan da Cunha Island. Lat37.03S Long12.18W Only settlement on the tiny island in the south Atlantic halfway between Capetown and Buenos Aires. Named in honour of Prince Alfred, the then Duke of Edinburgh.

Edinburgh USA Virginia. Lat38.50N Long78.36W

Edinburgh, Mount Australia. Queensland. Lat25.15S Long145.20E.

Eildon Hills Scotland Borders Lat55.35N Long2.43W 1.5 miles south of Melrose. Rise to three summits measuring 1,327ft, 1,385ft and 1,216ft. Contain the remains of a Roman encampment and a tumulus, believed to have been of Druidical origin.

Eildon Australia Victoria. The town in central Victoria was originally called Eildon Weir, the latter word referring to the dam that was built over the Goulburn river here to create a reservoir. The main port of the name was transferred from the Eildon Hills near Melrose in southern Scotland. Lake Eildon is a man made lake used for watersports.

Elderslie Scotland. *pop.* 5,286 (1991) Village 2 miles westof Paisley which is the traditionally regarded as the birthplace of Scottish patriot, William Wallace.

Elderslie Canada Ontario.

Elgin Scotland. Lat57.39N Long3.19W *pop.* 19,027 (1991). Capital of the former county of Moray. Royal burgh 37 miles east of Inverness.

Elgin USA Illinois. *pop.* 44,223 (1950) Industrial city in north east of state on the Cook-Cane county line on Fox River. With a name like this, there are several possible origins including the Scottish town of Elgin or one of the Earls of Elgin who took their title from it. There is a third possibility which is that the name derives from a hymn. The traditional account is that one of the founders, a devout Scotsman named James T Gifford, gave the name after his favourite hymn, *The Song of Elgin*. The town was founded in 1835, incorporated in 1847 and achieved city status in 1854. The city is now a centre for the printing of religious publications.

Elgin Canada Ontario. *pop.* c.300 (1950) Elgin, Ontario is probably named after James Bruce, Governor General of Canada 1847-1854. 30 miles north east of Kingston.

Elgin Canada Manitoba. *pop.* c.

400 (1950) Lies in south west of state on Elgin Creek 30 miles SSW of Brandon.

Elgin Canada New Brunswick. Elgin, New Brunswick is probably named after James Bruce, Governor General of Canada 1847-1854.

Elgin USA Iowa. *pop.* 642 (1950) Town in Fayette county in north east of state on Turkey River.

Elgin USA Kansas. *pop.* 212 (1950) City in south east Kansas in Chautauqua county on Caney River, 40 miles east of Arkansas.

Elgin USA Minnesota. *pop.* 438 (1950) Lies in Wabasha county in south east of state, 13 miles northeast of Rochester.

Elgin USA Nebraska. *pop.* 820 (1950) Village in Antelope county in north east central Nebraska on branch of Elkhorn River.

Elgin USA North Dakota. *pop.* 882 (1950) City in south of state in Grant county.

Elgin USA Ohio. *pop.* 126 (1950) Village in Van Wert county, 10 miles south east of Van Wert in west Ohio.

Elgin USA Oklahoma. *pop.* 428 (1950) Town in Commanche County in south west of state.

Elgin USA Oregon. *pop.* 1,223 (1950) City in Union County in north east Oregon on Grande Ronde River at an altitude of 2,670ft.

Elgin USA Pennsylvania. *pop.* 202 (1950) Borough in Erie County in north west of state.

Elgin USA Texas. *pop.* 3,168 (1950) City in Bastrop County. Settled 1867, incorporated 1890.

Elgin County Canada Ontario. *pop.* 46,000 (1950) Elgin County, Ontario is probably named after James Bruce, 8th Earl of Elgin (1811-1863), Governor General of Canada 1847-1854. Situated on the Thames River beside Lake Erie in southern Ontario. Capital of county is St Thomas.

Elgin Falls Sri Lanka.

Elie Scotland Fife. Lat56.12N Long2.49W *pop.* 903 (1991). Royal burgh situated on the Fife coast, 5 miles south east of Largo.

Elie Canada Manitoba.

Elie de Beumont New Zealand South Island. A mountain in west central South Island, 10,200ft in Southern Alps.

Falkland Scotland Fife. Lat56.15N Long3.12W *pop.* 1,197 (1991). Small town and ancient royal burgh. Location of Falkland Palace, a stronghold of the Stuarts.

Falkland Islands South Atlantic. The Falkland Islands are situated hundreds of miles away from Scotland close to the Antarctic where Captain John Strong, an English sailor, made the first recorded landing in 1690 and named the sound between the two main islands Falkland Sound, after Anthony Cary, 5th Viscount Falkland (1656-1694), Treasurer of the Navy from 1681-1689, and First Lord of the Admiralty subsequently. The name 'Falklands Lane' is first recorded in the log of Captain Woodes Rodgers, who visited the island in 1708 and the name 'Falklands Islands' was given when he took possession of the group in 1765. (Byran later renamed Falkland Sound as Carlisle Sound in honour of Charles Howard, 3rd Earl of Carlisle,who was First Lord of the Treasury in 1701 and again in 1715 but the name did not last. Viscount Falkland's title does come from the Scottish borough, however and was granted to the Cary family in 1620 by James VI of Scotland (James I of England).

Fife Scotland.
pop. c380,000 This self-containined peninsular county on Scotland's east coast is often referred to as the Kingdom of Fife. In the pre-industrial period Fife contained three of Scotland's imporrtant towns at Dunfermline, St Andrews and Falkland. Formerly a coal mining area. Now electronics and light industry.

Fife Lake USA Michigan. Village in Grand Traverse County, north west Michigan, on small Fife Lake. 18 miles south east of Traverse City.

Fife USA Texas. *pop.* c.24 (1996) Situated in the north part of McCulloch County. The area was first settled by the family of Alexander Mitchell and James Finlay, who were born in Scotland. The Mitchell family bought the land where Fife now lies and sold it in tracts. The name Fife was chosen by Mrs Agnes Finley, wife of James Finley from the county of her birth in Scotland when the town's post office was opened in 1902.

Lauderdale Scotland Borders. Long 55.45N Lat 2.45W Ancient district in west of Berwickshire.

Fort Lauderdale USA Florida.

Fort William Scotland. Lat56.49N Long5.06W *pop.* 10,391 (1991). Small town at the foot of Ben Nevis on east side of Loch Linnhe. The town has a couple of distilleries.

Fort William Canada Ontario. Lat48.23 N Long89.16W *pop.* 30,585 (1950) The city in Ontario lies on Thunder Bay, on the north west shore of Lake Superior, at the mouth of Kaministikwia River just south of its twin city of Port Arthur.

Fort William Cape Antarctica.
Lat62.26S Long59.45W

Fraserburgh Scotland
Aberdeenshire. *pop.* 12,843
(1991). Town with a strong
fishing tradition and is the site
of a coastguard and lifeboat
station.

Fraserburg South Africa.
Lat31.35S Long21.3 E.

Gifford Scotland East Lothian.
Lat55.54N Long3.02W *pop.*
688 (1991). Village 21 miles
east of Edinburgh.

Gifford USA Florida. *pop.* 1,459
(1950) Indian River County,
eastern Florida, just north of
Vero beach.

Gifford USA Iowa.

Gifford USA Missouri. *pop.* 16
(1950) Macon County, North
central Missouri. Situated on
the Chariton River, 23 miles
NNW of Macon.

Gifford USA South Carolina.
Hampton, South Carolina. 12
miles SSE of Allendale.
Industry includes lumber and
vegetable seeds.

Gifford USA Washington.

Glamis Scotland. Lat56.37N
Long3.00W Parish and village
5.5 miles south west of Forfar.
Pronounced Glams. Glamis
Castle is situated here.

Glamis Canada Saskatchewan.

Glasgo USA Connecticut.
Lat41.33 N Long71.53 W One
of two villages in town of
Griswold, New London
County on Quinebang River.
pop. of Griswold in 1950 was

5,728. Settled c.1690. City
incorporated 1895. Industries
of area include textiles,
agriculture, (poultry, fruit &
truck).

Glasco USA Kansas. *pop.* 803
(1950) City in Cloud County
Kansas. Industries include
flour and dairy products. Lies
on Solomon River in North
Central Kansas. Settled in
1799 and named by Scots
settlers but the first
postmaster spelt the name
incorrectly and it has never
been changed since.

Glasco USA New York. *pop.*
c.1,000 (1950) Village in
Ulster County New York.
Manufacturing of clothing &
brick. 8 miles above Kingston
on west bank of the Hudson.

Glasgow Scotland. Lat55.52N
Long4.15W *pop.* 662,954
(1991) Scotland's largest city,
which for the past three
centuries has been Scotland's
manufacturing and
commercial capital – known
in the industrial era as 'the
workshop of the world' or
'the second city of Empire'
because of its heavy
concentration of trading,
shipbuilding and engineering.
Although Kentigern or St
Mungo is believed to have
built a church on the site
where Glasgow Cathedral
now stands during the sixth
century, the first real mention
of the settlement was not

until 1124 when David I installed his chaplain, John Achaius as Bishop. Glasgow's heavy industrial demeanour has changed and its dense population has declined dramatically in recent decades.

Glasgow Guiana. Lat63.1N Long58.17W

Glasgow Jamaica. Lat18.21N Long78.13W *pop.* c.200 (1995) Tiny community in St Elizabeth Parish which is described as a farming community east of White Hill.

Glasgow Jamaica West Mooreland Parish.

Glasgow USA Kentucky. Lat36.59 N Long85.56W *pop.* 12,351 (1990) Situated in an oil and gas producing region. Other industries include timber, tobacco and grains.

Glasgow USA Missouri. Lat39.14N Long92.48W *pop.* 1,440 (1950) Howard County Missouri. City laid out in 1836, incorporated 1845. Industries include ships, grain, cattle and canning. This town was not named after Glasgow, Scotland but after a man called James Glasgow who helped establish the town in 1836.

Glasgow USA Montana. Lat48.12N Long106.37W *pop.* 3,572 (1990). Established in 1887 during the construction of the Great Northern Railway. The town is a centre for production of livestock, spring wheat and poultry.

Glasgow USA West Virginia. Lat37.38N Long79.29W *pop.* 810 (1950) Town in Rockbridge County W Virginia. Has large carpet mill and brick manufacturing. Lies on North River near its mouth on the James.

Glasgow USA West Virginia. Kanawha County West Virginia on Kanawha River. Town is in a coalmining region.

Glasgow USA Illinois. *pop.* 158 (1950) Village in Scoot county, west central Illinois. Agricultural area.

Glasgow (or Smiths Ferry) USA Pennsylvania. *pop.* c.70 (1994) Borough in Beaver county, Pennsylvania on Ohio River. The town which once had a population of 3,000 now has around 70 inhabitants. Laid out in 1836 and soared due to the discovery of oil deposits and once boasted an oil rig in nearly every back garden in the community.

Glasgow (now called Park City) USA Kentucky. Barren County, S Kentucky. Town was called Glasgow Junction until 1938. Lies 10 miles NW of Glasgow, Kentucky. Tourist centre for limestone cave region. SE gateway to Mammoth Cave National Park. Diamond Caverns, small caves nearby.

Glencoe Scotland. Long 56.14N Lat 5.06W Glen in north Argyllshire on Coe River which flows to Loch Leven. Famous for the massacre of MacDonalds of Glen Coe which occured in February 1792.

Glencoe Canada Nova Scotia. Prince Edward Island. Believed to have been named by a Scot known only as Mr A Macdonald.

Glencoe Canada Ontario. Believed to have been named by the same Mr Macdonald as for Glencoe, Nova Scotia.

Glencoe South Africa.

Glencoe USA Illinois. *pop.* 8,499 (1991). Village in Cook county on Lake Michegan which is residential suburb of Chicago. The Chicago Botanic Gardens are based in Glencoe.

Glencoe USA Minnesota. Martin McLeod named it after the famous glen in Scotland.

Glenelg Scotland Inverness-shire. Lat57.13N Long5.37W Estate and village which is 7 miles south west of Lochalsh.

Glenelg Australia.

Glenorchy Scotland. Lat56.28N Long4.51W Glenorchy and Inishail is a united parish 12 miles west of Tyndrum.

Glenorchy Australia South Australia. The town in South Australia was first called

Bangor after either Bangor in Wales or Ireland but the name was changed by Alex Campbell, one of four brothers who had emigrated from Glenorchy, one of the Duke of Argyll's properties in Scotland from where they came.

Gourock Scotland Renfrewshire. Lat55.58N Long4.49N *pop.* 11,473 (1991) Situated on the south shore of Firth of Clyde, 2 miles below Greenock.

Gourock Range Australia. Lat35.45S Long149.25E. Mountain range.

Grampians Scotland. Mountain range which stretches the country forming a natural border between the highlands and lowlands.

Grampians Australia Victoria. Mountain range. Craggy sandstone ranges forming the western end of the great dividing range.

Grampian USA Pennsylvania. The community of Grampian, Pennsylvania, was named by Samuel Coleman in 1809 after the Grampian Mountains in Scotland where he came from.

Greenock Scotland Renfrewshire. Lat55.57N Long4.46W *pop.* 50,013 (1991) Seaport, manufacturing and former major shipbuilding town on the south shore of the Firth of Clyde. In the seventeenth century Greenock was just a small fishing village but due to the herring boom had 900 boats operating from the port by the 1760s. Greenock became a major passenger port from Ireland and the Scottish Highlands and to North America. Computer giants IBM are now one of the largest employers.

Greenock Canada Ontario.

Gretna Scotland Dumfries-shire . Lat54.60N Long3.04W *pop.* 3,149 (1991) Township on Solway Firth 9.5 miles north west of Carlisle.

Gretna USA Louisiana. *pop.* 17,208 (1991) Industries include manufacturing of cottonseed oil, asbestos, barrels and petroleum products. Originally known as Mechanickham when it was founded in the early 1800s. Renamed after the famous Gretna Green in Scotland, because an early justice of the peace here performed marriages twenty four hours a day without the need of a legal certificate, similar to the way that eloping English couples could get married without a licence in the Scottish village until 1856.

Gretna Canada Manitoba. This is a point of entry on the Manitoba-North Dakota border and it was so named by the Canadian Pacific Railway in 1883 because the

Scottish Gretna Green is similarly near the border with England.

Haliburton Scotland.

Haliburton Canada Ontario

Hamilton Scotland Lanarkshire. Lat55.47N Long4.02W *pop.* 49,991 (1991). Situated on the confluence of Avon and Clyde rivers, 11.5 miles south east of Glasgow. Originally called Cadzow, a name which still attaches to the sixteenth century castle ruins. The town was formerly a coal mining area.

Hamilton Australia New South Wales. Western suburb of Newcastle in south of state.

Hamilton Australia Tasmania. Village in south central Tasmania.

Hamilton Australia Victoria. Lat37.45 S Long 142.04E Situated in south west of county. 160 miles west of Melbourne. Near to Dunkeld and Grampians.

Hamilton Bermuda. Lat 32.18N Long 64.44 W *pop.* c.3,000 (1949) Capital city and chief port of Bermuda on Bermuda Island. Town is laid out in triangular fashion running along one mile of coast. Incorporated in 1790 and succeeded St George as capital in 1815. It is a tourist centre. There is also a Hamilton parish in east Bermuda surrounding Harrington Sound.

Hamilton Canada Ontario. Lat 43.15N Long 79.50W *pop.* 318,499 (1991) Capital city of Wentworth County in southern Ontario on Hamilton Harbour at head of Lake Ontario. Laid out in 1813 by George Hamilton and was in the same year the scene for the battle of Stoney Creek.

Hamilton New Zealand North Island. Lat37.48S Long175.18E Borough in the north of North Island which lies in, but is independent of, Waikato county.

Hamilton Sierra Leone. *pop.* 231 (1931) A village and minor port on Atlantic Ocean on Sierra Leone Peninsula. Platinum mining area.

Hamilton USA Alaska.

Hamilton USA Georgia.

Hamilton USA Illinois.

Hamilton USA Indiana.

Hamilton USA Iowa.

Hamilton USA Kansas.

Hamilton USA Massachusetts.

Hamilton USA Montana.

Hamilton USA Nebraska.

Hamilton USA New Jersey *pop.* 86,553 (1990) Situated in Mercer County, west central New Jersey.

Hamilton USA Nevada.

Hamilton USA New York. *pop.* 6,221 (1990) Situated in Madison County, central New York.

Hamilton USA North Carolina.

Hamilton USA North Dakota.

Hamilton USA North Virginia.

Hamilton USA Ohio. Lat 39.23N Long84.33W *pop.* 61,368 (1990) Seat of Butler County, south west Ohio on Great Miami River. Pioneer settlement took place around Fort Hamilton as early as 1791. The fort was intended to keep homesteaders safe from Indian attacks. Incorporated 1810.

Hamilton USA Rhode Island

Hamilton USA Tennessee.

Hamilton USA Texas.

Hamilton USA Washington.

Hamilton Acres USA Alaska. *pop.* c.214 (1950) Village in west of state near Yukon River delta.

Hamilton Air Force Base USA California.

Hamilton Beach Canada Ontario. Village resort in south Ontario and western suburb of Hamilton.

Hamilton, Cape Australia Northwest Territories. Situated on south west of Victoria Island.

Hamilton City USA California. *pop.* 703 (1940) Village in Glenn county in north central California.

Hamilton County USA Florida. *pop.* 8,981 (1950) County covering 514 sq miles in north Florida whose county seat is Jasper. On Georgia line and bounded by Suwannee River to the south and east and Withlacoochie River to the west. Flatwoods area with swamps in east. Formed in 1827.

Hamilton County USA Texas.

Hamilton Cove Canada Quebec. *pop.* c.800 (1950) This village is also known is Sainte Anne de Portneuf. Lies in east of state on the St Lawrence.

Hamilton Dam USA Texas.

Hamilton Field USA California. (See Hamilton Air Force Base)

Hamilton, Fort USA New York.

Hamilton Inlet Canada Labrador. Bay at inlet of the Atlantic, south east Labrador. Outlet of Lake Melville which is 50 miles wide at entrance.

Hamilton, Lake USA Arkansas.

Hamilton, Lake USA Florida

Hamilton, Lake USA Texas.

Hamilton Lakes USA North Carolina. *pop.* c.900 (1950) Town in Guilford County north central North Carolina. Residential suburb of Greensboro.

Hamilton, Mount USA California. Peak in western California.

Hamilton Range USA California Part of Diablo Range 4,372 ft. On summit is Lick Observatory of University of California.

Hamilton, Mount USA Nevada.

Hamilton River Canada Newfoundland. Lat 53.20 N Long 60.00 W

Helensburgh Scotland Dunbartonshire. This seaside town became popular with Glasgow merchants towards the end of the eighteenth century. Henry Bell the steamship pioneer kept a hotel in Helensburgh, the need for patrons, it is thought acting as an incentive to develop fast and efficient water transport on the Clyde. Also the birthplace of television inventor John Logie Baird, Helensburgh is a quiet residential town popular with Glasgow commuters.

Helensburgh New Zealand. Now situated in the new City of Dunedin boundary due to local government reorganisation in 1989. It is likely to have been named after the coastal town on the Firth of Clyde, Scotland.

Heriot Scotland Midlothian. Long55.46N Lat2.59W Parish in south east Midlothian on Heriot Water.

Heriot New Zealand.

Highland USA California *pop.* 34,439 (1990) City in San Bernardino County in foothills of San Bernardino mountains.

Highland USA Illinois. The city of Highland in Illinois was named specifically after the Highlands of Scotland by Scottish settlers. Residents are mainly of Swiss and German heritage. The town claims to be home of the Swiss national anthem.

Highland USA Indiana. *pop.* 23,696 (1990)

Highland USA Pennsylvania.

Houston Scotland Renfrewshire.

Houston USA Texas. City and port connected to Gulf of Mexico by a 94km canal. It is often called Space City as the Lyndon B Johnson Space Centre is nearby. Not named after Houston, Renfrewshire but was founded in 1836 and named after General Sam Houston (1793–1863) who won Texan independence from Mexico. Houston is a major petroleum centre.

Huntly Scotland Aberdeenshire. Lat57.27N Long2.48W *pop.* 4,230 (1990) Town in Strath Bogie at confluence of Bogie and Deveron, 41 miles north west of Aberdeen. Huntly is also a former village in Berwickshire. It was an estate of the Gordons who on removal to the north gave the same name to this place in Aberdeenshire.

Huntly New Zealand North Island. The town in North Island was named by an early settler after his native town in Scotland. The Maori name of the town is Rahuipuketo, said to mean 'Sanctuary of Swampbirds'.

Inverness Scotland. Lat57.29N Long4.14W *pop.* 41,234 (1991). Royal and municipal burgh and capital of the northern Highlands. Situated at the north east of the Caledonian Canal on River Ness near the confluence with Inner Moray Firth. Inverness has grown in size in recent years due to the influence of North Sea oil exploration and is a major centre for the many thousands of visitors to the Scottish Highlands.

Inverness Canada Cape Breton Island. Lat46.14 N Long61.19W *pop.* c.3,000 West coast of Cape Breton Island on Northumbrian Strait. It is a coal mining and coal shipping port.

Inverness Canada Quebec. Lat46.15N Long71.34W *pop.* c.220 (1950) County seat of Megantic County S Quebec.

Inverness USA California. Lat38.06N Long122.5W

Inverness USA Florida. Lat28.51N Long82.21W *pop.* c.1,500 (1950) County seat of Citrus County central Florida. According to local history books this town was named after 'a lonely Scot' who was reminded of his home town.

Inverness USA Illinois. *pop.* 1,200 (1994) Cook county, NE Illinois. Northwestern suburb of Chicago situated thirty miles from the Chicago Loop which was originally designed as a getaway for young families, but is now an exclusive residential area.

Inverness USA Mississippi. Lat33.21N Long90.40W *pop.* c.1,000 (1950) The town in

Sunflower County Mississippi is a rich cotton growing area.

Inverness USA Montana Lat48.33N Long110.40W

Inverness County Canada Canada Cape Breton Island. *pop.* c.21,000 (1947) County is 1,409 squ miles. County seat is Port Hood. East of Cape Breton Island on Gulf of St Lawrence.

Iona Scotland. Lat56.20N Long6.25W Small island and village in the Inner Hebrides off the south west coast of Mull. Iona was an early Christian centre established by St Columba. The impressive Iona Abbey attracts many visitors and pilgrims and is the burial ground of 48 Scottish kings including Kenneth MacAlpine and Macbeth.

Iona Canada Nova Scotia. Situated on Prince Edward Island

Iona Canada Ontario.

Iona Canada Cape Breton Island

Irvine Scotland Ayrshire. Lat55.37N Long4.40W *pop.* 32,988 (1991) Royal and municipal burgh in Ayrshire near mouth of River Irvine, 7 miles west of Kilmarnock.

Irvine USA California. *pop.* 110,330 (1990) City situated in Orange County, southwest California which was created in the 1970s as a planned community and continues to expand rapidly.

Irvine USA Kentucky. County seat of Estill County on Kentucky River.

Irving USA Illinois. Situated in Montgomery county.

Irving USA Kansas. Situated in Marshall county on Big Blue River.

Irving USA Texas. Town and suburb of Dallas.

Islay Scotland Argyll. Lat55.46N Long6.09W Island 13 miles west of Kintyre. It measure 25 miles across and 19 miles long at its widest points. Famous for its distinctive malt whiskies.

Islay Canada Alberta. Until 1907 this community was known as Island Lake but the name was changed by one of the many Scots who settled here.

Islay Province Peru. *pop.* 25,691. Capital of province is Mollendo. Situated in irrigation area for rice, sugar, cotton, grain and fruit. Industries include textile and flour mills, bottling plant, shoe and furniture factories, fish canneries, distilleries. The main export is Alpace wool.

Jedburgh Scotland Roxburghshire. Lat55.29N Long2.33W *pop.* 4,118 (1991). Royal Burgh situated on Jed Water, 10 miles south west of Kelso. Once the county town of Roxburghshire which grew around the medieval abbey.

Jedburgh Canada Saskatchewan.

Johnstone Scotland
Renfrewshire. Lat55.50N
Long4.30W *pop.* 18,635
(1991) The town grew from a
population of 10 in 1781 to
over 7000 in 1841 due to the
development of cotton
spinning, then coal mining
and engineering.
Johnstone Canada Ontario.
Kelso Scotland Roxburghshire.
Lat55.36N Long2.26W *pop.*
5,989 (1991) Because of close
proximity to England the
town's history is turbulent. It
was burned on no less than
three occasions between
1523 and 1545. Kelso Abbey
never recovered from the
third attack.
Kelso Canada Saskatchewan.
Kelso New Zealand.
Kelso USA California.
Kelso USA Missouri. *pop.* 276
(1950) Scott County SE
Missouri. It is near the
Mississippi River, 3 miles SW
of Illmo.
Kelso USA North Dakota.
Kelso USA Washington. *pop.*
11,820 (1990) Settlement
used as early as 1840 by
Hudson Bay Company fur
traders. The city of Kelso is
the county seat of Cowlitz
County, Washington. It was
settled in 1847 by a Scottish
surveyor, Peter Crawford,
who named it after his native
town of Kelso,
Roxburghshire. It was
incorporated as a town in

1889 and as a city in 1908. It
became the county seat in
1932. It lies on the Cowlitz
River.
Kildonan Scotland Sutherland.
Lat57.30N Long6.25W The
Helmsdale River runs through
the Strath of Kildonan for
over twenty miles. The valley
was named after a saint
believed to have been of
Pictish background, educated
at Whithorn and murdered
on the Isle of Eigg in 617AD.
The population in 1811 was
over 1500. However this had
plummeted to 157 in twenty
years, mainly due to
emigration. The then
Countess of Sutherland was
responsible for the clearance
after threatening the families
of young men who would not
enlist in her regiment that
they would be replaced by
sheep.
Kildonan Canada Manitoba. This
is now a suburban area of
Winnipeg, Manitoba, situated
on both sides of the Red
River and known as East
Kildonan and West Kildonan.
Its rural districts are known
as Old Kildonan and North
Kildonan. The community
was founded by the Scottish
philanthropist Thomas
Douglas, 5th Earl of Selkirk, in
1817, when he named after
the village of Kildonan,
Sutherland, from where a
number of settlers had

emigrated. Selkirk took a party of 100 of the 700 who had applied for grants of land in his settlement each paying £10. They sailed from Stromness on the *Prince of Wales* in convoy with the *Eddystone* which carried servants and officials.

Kildonan Zimbabwe.

Kilmarnock Scotland Ayrshire. Lat55.36N Long4.30W *pop.* 44,307 (1991) According to folklore Kilmarnock owes its existence to a missionary named Mernoc or Marnoc who settled here in the seventh century. Little is known of Kilmarnock until the fourteenth century when the Boyd family were given land for their part in the battle of Bannockburn. They became suzerains of Kilmarnock and their home was Dean Castle.

Kilmarnock USA Virginia Lat37.43N Long76.24W *pop.* 689 (1950) Lancaster and Northumberland counties E Virginia, near Chesapeake Bay. Nearby Christ Church was built in 1732. Industries include fisheries, lumber mills, canneries.

Kilsyth Scotland Stirlingshire. Lat55.59N Long4.60W *pop.* 9,918 (1991) Town is 12 miles north east of Glasgow. The nearby ruins of Kilsyth Castle was the family seat of the Viscounts of Kilsyth. Scene of

the battle of Kilsyth in 1645 where James Graham Marquis of Montrose won his last battle.

Kilsyth USA West Virginia. *pop.* c.400 (1994) The community of Kilsyth, West Virginia, was named after the Scottish town in Stirlingshire from where some of the original settlers had come.

Kincardine-on-Forth Scotland Fife. Lat56.04N Long3.43W *pop.* 3,184 (1991) Once a detached section of Perthshire which once contained salt pans for the extraction of salt from sea water. Later, during the eighteenth and nineteenth centuries it became a busy Forth port and shipbuilding centre second only to Leith. This industry fell away and now the Forth River at Kincardine is the home to two power stations. Kincardine Bridge was the most easterly bridge between Edinburgh and Fife until the opening of the Forth Road Bridge in 1964.

Kincardine Canada Ontario. *pop.* 6,585 (1990) Village situated in south of state in Bruce County, by Lake Huron and 45 miles SW of Owen Sound. Knitting and woollen mills, furniture factory and salt works are among the local industries.The town is also a resort. Named after

Kincardine-of-Forth. The nearby Bruce Nuclear Power Development is the major employer.

Kingham Scotland.

Kingham Canada Ontario.

Kinloch House Scotland Perthshire. Lat56.32N Long3.46W

Kinloch USA Missouri. The city of Kinloch, Missouri, was settled by a Scottish family, who had an estate of this name in Virginia, and who thus named both the estate and the settlement after their native village of Kinloch, possibly the one near Blairgowrie, Perthshire.

Kinross Scotland Kinross-shire. Lat56.12N Long3.25W *pop.* 4,552 (1991). Small town on the western shore of Loch Leven adjacent to Loch Leven castle. The only burgh when Kinross-shire was a county. Kinross-shire was the second smallest county in Scotland before local government reorganisation in 1975.

Kinross Australia Western Australia. Place situated on Burns Beach (named after Robert Burns) that lies 30 mins north of Perth.

Kinross South Africa Transvaal. The village of Kinross, in the Transvaal, was founded in 1910 and named after the Scottish town of Kinross from which many of the engineers

who constructed the railway here had come.

Kirriemuir Scotland Angus. Small town which was once the centre of handloom weaving and later jute processing. The birthplace of *Peter Pan* creator, J M Barrie whose home has now has been converted into a museum by the National Trust for Scotland.

Kirriemuir Canada Alberta.

Lanark Scotland Lanarkshire. Lat55.40N Long3.46W *pop.* 8,877 (1991) A royal burgh and once county town of Lanarkshire.

Lanark Australia Western Australia.

Lanark Canada Manitoba. District in Pipestone Valley, Manitoba. Nearby town called Reston.

Lanark Canada Ontario. *pop.* c.660 (1950) Situated in south east of Ontario on Clyde River ten miles NW of Perth. Economic activity includes knitting, lumber mills and dairying. Settled in 1820 by emigrants mainly from Lanarkshire but also from Dunbartonshire, Clackmannanshire and West Lothian who were allotted land in Lanark as well as Dalhousie and Ramsay. The people from Lanarkshire and Renfrewshire had drawn up petitions asking for aid for emigration. They were weavers.

Lanark USA Florida. Established as a holiday resort called Lanark-on-the-Gulf but was destroyed by a hurricane in 1929 and later rebuilt as an army training centre. The army training centre has now become a retirement village.

Lanark USA Illinois. *pop.* 1,359 (1950) Situated in Carroll County NW Illinois. Near Rock Creek, 17 miles SW of Freeport. Incorporated 1887. The community was named after the home town of the Scottish bankers who funded the building of a railroad through the town.

Lanark USA West Virginia The community of Lanark, West Virginia, was named for the town (or county, Lanarkshire) in Scotland, from where early settlers had emigrated.

Lanark County Canada Ontario. Lanark County, Ontario, was similarly named by early settlers in 1820. The seat of this county is Perth.

Leith Scotland Midlothian. This was Scotland's principal port in the mid nineteenth century importing and exporting goods such as grain, flax, sugar, timber, iron, paper and whisky. Shipbuilding became the largest employer in the seventeenth century. Leith became independent from Edinburgh in1833 when the cost of upkeep of the docks bankrupted Edinburgh. The

burgh amalgamated with Edinburgh in 1920 and is now a fashionable suburb of the Scots capital.

Leith Canada Ontario.

Leith USA Alabama.

Leith USA Arkansas.

Leith USA Nevada.

Leith USA North Dakota. Tiny village in Grant County in south of North Dakota

Leith USA Pennsylvania. Situated in Fayette County in SW of State.

Leith USA South Georgia.

Leith Valley New Zealand. Situated within the City of Dunedin boundary, South Island.

Leslie Scotland Aberdeenshire.

Leslie Scotland Fife. Long 56.12N Lat 3.13W *pop.* 3,062 (1991) Leslie was a prosperous flax and bleaching burgh which unlike surrounding towns was not part of the coal industry.

Leslie South Africa Transvaal. The village of Leslie in the Transvaal was proclaimed in 1939 and is believed to be named after one or other Scottish places of the name (either the town in Fife or the village near Huntly, Aberdeenshire). Settlers could well have come from either of these. It is more likely to have been named after the Fife town by two Patterson brothers who surveyed the railway line

between Springs and Bethal
during 1904 and 1906. They
are rumoured to have come
from Kinross, Scotland.
Leslie USA Arkansas. *pop.* 610
(1950) Town in Searcy County
N Arkansas whose main
industry is a cooperage.
Leslie USA Georgia. *pop.* 417
(1950) Sumter County SW
central Georgia. An
agricultural village. 12 miles
SE of Americus.
Leslie USA Idaho.
Leslie USA Michigan. *pop.* 1,543
(1950) Village in Ingham
County. Agricultural area, 14
miles N of Jackson (livestock,
poultry, fruit, grain,
sugarbeets, corn). Settled
1836, incorporated 1869.
Leslie USA Missouri. *pop.* 114
(1950) Town in Franklin
County. Situated in Ozark
region, 15 miles SW of
Washington.
Leslie County USA Kentucky.
pop. 15,537 (1950) County in
SE Kentucky covering 412
square miles and the seat of
the county is Hyden. It is
situated in a mountainous
agricultural area in the
Cumberlands. Corn, hay,
truck, livestock, fruit,
tobacco, timber and
bitumous coal mines are the
industries. Formed in 1878.
Leven Scotland Fife. Lat56.12N
Long2.60W *pop.* 8,317 (1991)
The village of Leven was
once a centre for linen

weaving on the banks of the
River Leven. In the
nineteenth century the
development of the coalfield
in the area changed the town
dramatically.
Leven South Africa Transvaal.
Town in the Transvaal named
by the Patterson brothers
who also named Leslie and
Kinross when they surveyed
the railway line between
Springs and Bethal in the
early 1900s. They are
believed to have came from
Kinross, Scotland.
Lismore Scotland Argyll.
Lat56.31N Long5.30W *pop.*
c.140 (1994) Picturesque
island in the southern end of
Loch Linnhe measuring 10
miles long by 1.5 miles wide.
The name derives from the
Gaelic words 'lios mor'
meaning 'Great Garden'
which was probably given to
the island by St Molauag who,
as legend has it, beat his rival
St Columba to the land by
cutting off his little finger and
throwing it ashore in the sixth
century. In 1775 there was an
emigration surge to North
Carolina in particular. By 1831
the population had fallen to
1497.
Lismore Australia New South
Wales. *pop.* c.33,000 (1994)
The city of Lismore in New
South Wales was settled in
1845 and most likely to be
named after the Scottish

island in Loch Linnhe for the area's original settler William Wilson who was a Scot. Largest town on the north coast of NSW.

Lochaber Scotland Inverness-shire. Lat57.00N Long5.12W The ancient lordship of Lochaber stretches north from Loch Leven to Glengarry and west from Badenoch to Moidart. The area was often the scene of confrontation between the Campbells and the MacDonalds.

Lochaber Canada Nova Scotia. It must have been Scottish emigrants here in Nova Scotia who chose the name of the Scottish Highland district and loch for the Canadian lake, and for the settlement that arose by it.

Lochgelly Scotland Fife. Lat56.01N Long3.19W *pop.* 7,044 (1991) Town in Fife 0.5 miles northwest of Loch Gelly.

Lochgelly USA West Virginia. The community in West Virginia was originally known as Stuart, a name given by Samuel Dixon, a coal operator, in honour of the royal house of Scotland. After a tragic mining accident in 1907, in which 84 men lost their lives, he changed the name to Lochgelly, after the Lochgelly Coal and Iron Company at the town of this name in Fife, which was owned by an associate of his. Dixon had experienced difficulties hiring new miners after the disaster so felt that a change of name would improve things.

Longa Island Scotland. Ross & Cromarty. Situated at the head of Gair Loch.

Longa River Angola. The river may be named after Longa Island, Scotland.

Lorn Scotland Argyll. Lat56.28N Long5.07W A district between the Lochs Leven, Awe, Avich and Melfort.

Lorne Australia Victoria. The town in South West Victoria was founded in 1871 as a coastal resort and was named by its Scottish settlers after the Firth of Lorn that lies to the east of it.

Melfort, Loch Scotland Argyll. Lat56.16N Long5.30W Sea loch in former Argyllshire. Melfort House is situated at north east head of loch.

Melfort Canada Saskatchewan. *pop.* 5,628 (1990) The town in Saskatchewan was originally known as Stoney Creek. In 1904 its name was changed to Melford, after the Scottish birthplace, Melford House, of an early settler, Mary Melford Campbell (married name Beatty).

Melrose Scotland Roxburghshire. Lat55.36N Long2.43W *pop.* 2,270 (1991) The first monastery at Melrose was founded by St Aiden in the seventh century which was deserted by the eleventh century. In the twelfth century David I encouraged Cisterian monks from Rievaulx to settle a new monastery at Melrose. They founded Melrose Abbey in 1136 which was soon to become one of the richest in Scotland. In the fourteenth century it was destroyed by Richard II and was replaced in the fifteenth century only to be destroyed in 1545. Excavations to the abbey in 1920s discovered a coffin which may have belonged to Waltheof and a cone-shaped lead container which contained a mummified heart which is believed to be that of Robert I who ordered his heart to be buried at Melrose.

Melrose Australia South Australia. *pop.* c.250 (1931) Situated 17 miles NNE of Port Pirie. The town was founded on the promise of rich mineral deposits and although a copper mine was established in 1846 it closed twelve years later after $20,000 was invested without any return.

Melrose Australia Western Australia.

Melrose Canada Nova Scotia.

Melrose USA Florida. *pop.* c.620 (1941) A village resort on the Alachuan-Putnam county line in northern Florida in citrus growing region.

Melrose USA Idaho.

Melrose USA Iowa. *pop.* c.310 (1950) Town in Monroe county south Iowa on Cedar Creek. Coal mining region.

Melrose USA Massachusetts. *pop.* 28,150 (1990) The city was settled in 1633, originally as part of Charlestown. After two further changes of the name (North Malden, Pond Feilde), it became Melrose, after the Scottish town. It lies in Middlesex county 7 miles north of Boston.

Melrose USA Minnesota. Situated in Stearns County in central Minnesota on Sauk River. It was settled in 1857 and incorporated as city in 1898.

Melrose USA Montana. *pop.* c.300 (1950) Village in Silver Bow county, south west Montana on the Big Hole River. It is a livestock region.

Melrose USA New Mexico. *pop.* c.1,000 (1950) Village in Curry county in east New Mexico.

Melrose USA New York Residential district in south Bronx which is a business centre for a black and Hispanic community.

Melrose USA Ohio. *pop.* c.230 (1950) Village in Paulding county in north west Ohio.

Melrose USA Oregon.

Melrose USA Wisconsin. *pop.* c.500 (1950) Village in

Jackson county, central Wisconsin. Limestone quaries nearby.

Melrose Park USA Illinois. *pop.* 10,859 (1990) Residential village and suburb of Chicago in Cook County. Incorporated 1893.

Melrose Park USA New York. *pop.* 1,800 (1950) Village in Cayuga County.

Melrose Park USA Pennsylvania. Village in Montgomery County.

Melsetter Scotland Orkney. Lat58.47N Long3.16W Place on Hoy Island at head of Long Hope, 18 miles southwest of Kirkwall.

Melsetter Zimbabwe. The town of this name is now known as Chimmanimani. It was founded in 1893 by two Scottish trekkers from the Orange Free State, South Africa, whose names were Thomas and Dunbar Moodie and who came from the Melsetter in the Orkneys. On the independence of Zimbabwe in 1980, the name was changed to Mandidzwzure. Two years later it was further changed to Chimanimani.

Midlothian Scotland. Former county of which the city of Edinburgh was the centre. Sometimes referred to as Edinburghshire.

Midlothian USA Illinois. *pop.* 14,372 (1990) Residential

suburb of Chicago. The town was so designated not so much from the former Scottish county but as a literary tribute to Sir Walter Scott, in particular his novel *The Heart of Midlothian* published in 1818.

Minto Scotland Roxburghshire. Lat55.29N Long2.40W Village in former Roxburghshire on River Teviot. Nearby Minto House is the seat of the Earl of Minto.

Minto Canada New Brunswick. *pop.* 3,096 (1990) Possibly named in honour of Gilbert John Elliot Murray Kynynmound, 4th Earl of Minto (1845-1914), who was Governor General of Canada 1898-1904. The earl gets his title from his family seat, Minto House, at the Scottish village of this name near Jedburgh.

Moffat Scotland Dumfries-shire. Lat55.20N Long3.27W *pop.* 2,342 (1991) Once situated on the main road from Scotland to England but now bypassed by the M74 motorway. Became a royal burgh in 1648. By the mid eighteenth century the town became a popular attraction. With the arrival of the railway the springs lost out to others that were more remote.

Moffat USA Colorado. *pop.* 109 (1950) Town in Saguache County. Shipping point in livestock region on San Luis Creek, 14 miles ESE of Saguache. At an altitude of 7,564 ft.

Moffat County USA Colorado. *pop.* c.6,000 (1950) County in extreme north west of Colorado. County seat is Craig. Formed in 1911. Livestock grazing area, includes National Forest area.

Moffat Tunnel USA Colorado. North Central Colorado. 6.4 miles long at altitude of around 9,000 ft. Pioneer bore (8ft. in diameter, built 1923-27) used to carry water to Denver. Second bore (24ft high, 18ft wide, finished 1928) is used by railroad.

Montrose Scotland Angus Lat56.44N Long2.25W *pop.* 11,440 (1991) Located on the North Sea at the mouth of the River Esk. The name derives from Gaelic and means 'a moor on peninsula'. The town's castle was destroyed in 1297 by William Wallace and never rebuilt. Montrose became a Royal Burgh during the reign of David II, and prospered due to its harbour and trading links. Today the town is a holiday resort with golf courses and Montrose Basin, a nature reserve.

Montrose USA Arkansas. Town lies in Ashley county.

Montrose USA California. Unincorporated town in county of Los Angeles in foothills of San Gabriel Mountains. 11 miles north of downtown Los Angeles.

Montrose USA Colorado. Lat38.29 N Long107.53 *pop.* 8,854 (1990) County seat in western Colorado.It lies at an altitude of 5,820 ft on Uncompahgre River. Nearby carnotie deposits are a source of Radium and Uranium. Founded and named in 1882.

Montrose USA Georgia. Town in Laurens County 15 miles west of Dublin.

Montrose USA Illinois. Village in Effingham County.

Montrose USA Iowa. Town in Lee County in the extreme south east of state on Mississippi River. One of the first permenant settlements in Iowa was established here when Louis Tesson, a French Canadian established a trading post. Town was laid out in 1837.

Montrose USA Michegan. Village in Genesee County.

Montrose USA Minnesota. Village in Wright County.

Montrose USA Mississippi. Town in Jasper County

Montrose USA Montana. City in Henry County.

Montrose USA Pennsylvania. Borough and seat of Susquehanna County in north east of state. Mountain resort settled in 1799, incorporated 1824.

Montrose USA South Dakota. City in McCook County in south east of state.

Montrose USA Texas. *pop.* 12,341 (1990) Residential section of Houston which is regarded as the most Bohemian district with ongoing restoration of early 20th century housing.

Montrose USA Virginia. Village in Randolph County.

Montrose County USA Colorado. Seat of county is also called Montrose.

Moscow Scotland Ayrshire. Village north east of Kilmarnock.

Mossgiel Scotland Ayrshire. The Ayrshire farm where poet Robert Burns lived for four years. While he lived at the farm Burns had his first volume of poems published titled *Poems, Chiefly in the Scottish Dialect*.

Mosgiel New Zealand South Island. The town of Mosgiel, in South Island, was given the name of the Scottish farm by an early settler here, a colleague of William Cargill (who gave his name to InverCargill), and who like him was a leading member of the ScottishFree Church and of the colonising community.

Musselburgh Scotland East Lothian. Seaside town on the River Forth near Edinburgh. The old town dates back to before the fourteenth century. Originally called Eskmouth but renamed after a mussel bank near the mouth of the River Esk.

Musselburgh New Zealand. Place name within the City of Dunedin boundary. Named after Musselburgh, Scotland.

Nairn Scotland Nairnshire. Lat57.35N Long3.52W *pop.* 7,892 (1991) Its ancient name is Invernairn. It is one of the earliest burghs in the northeast of Scotland, having been in existence since 1214. The medieval castle was destroyed in the sixteenth century. Was a fishing port until the collapse of the herring industry in 1920s, and the silting of the harbour mouth. Today Nairn is a holiday resort and residential area.

Nairn Canada Ontario.

Nevis Island Central America. Lat17.11N Long62.35W May be named after Ben Nevis or Loch Nevis Scotland.

New Annan Canada Nova Scotia. The community in Nova Scotia was founded in about 1806 by a Scottish emigrant from Annandale, Scotland. They were later followed by other families from Annandale. It is situated on the Northumbrian Strait. New Annan is a rural community with no real industry.

Newburgh Scotland Fife. Lat56.21N Long3.14W *pop.*

2,032 (1991) Situated on the Firth of Tay opposite Mugdrum Island, thecommunity owes its existence to Lindores Abbey. Up until 1898 linoleum and weaving were the prominent industries

Newburgh USA Indiana. *pop.* 2,880 (1990) Situated in Warrick County on the Ohio River.

Newburgh USA New York. *pop.* 26,454 (1990) Situated in Orange County, the settlement took its present name in 1752 during an influx of Scots and English settlers. Was originally settled by Germans in 1709 but then became a Parish in 1752 and was named after the Scottish town of Newburgh, Fife. There may well have been emigrant Scottish connections, but of course the name does mean (New Borough) in its own right.

New Caledonia Pacific Ocean. A French overseas territory, named by James Cook in 1774. He chose the Roman name of Scotland as a complement to the nearby New Hebrides (now Vanuata) which he had named not so long before. New Britain and New Ireland lay further to the north in what later came to be called the Bismark Archipelago. Cook had already used Wales for New

South Wales so all four constituents of the British Isles came to be represented in new form on the map. The French never renamed it possibly because their hold over the islands has never been strong, and in recent years (especially since 1984) there have been increasing demands by the Melanesians for self government.

New Dundee Canada Ontario. *pop.* c.400 (1950) Village which was named in 1830 by John Millar who came to Canada with his two brothers from Dundee, Scotland.

New Edinburgh Canada Ottawa. Lat45.28N Long75.42W

New Edinburg USA Arkansas. Lat33.46 N Long92.16 W

New Glasgow Canada Nova Scotia. *pop.* 9,905 (1990) The town was founded in 1809, incorporated 1875. Founded after the discovery of coal deposits locally some ten years earlier. It was named after the Scottish city by Scots settlers, and in particular one William Fraser, who surveyed the site and foresaw 'another Clyde and another Glasgow'. (The'Clyde' is actually called the East River here) Town was settled in 1819 by distressed weavers.

New Hebrides Pacific Ocean. A chain of islands in the southwest Pacific, west of Fiji, where they are currently jointly administered by France and Britain. They were initially discovered by the Portuguese in 1606, were rediscovered by the French in 1768, andsix years later were charted and named by James Cook after the Scottish Islands. He felt that the appearance of the jagged rocksand crags on the islands were similar to those of the Hebrides in his native land.

New Scotland USA New York. The New York community was settled and named by Scotsmen.

New Scotland South Africa Transvaal. The region of New Scotland was settledby Scottish immigrants. The head settlement was later named Roburnia, after the Scottish national poet, Robert Burns, although this name was soon changed to Amsterdam with Dutch loyalties gaining the upper hand over the Scottish.

Nith River Scotland. Rises 3 miles east of Dalmellington and flows 9 miles east to New Cumnock, Ayrshire then 70 miles into the Solway Firth.

Nith River Canada Ontario. Named after the Scottish river in Dumfriesshire by James Jackson, one of the founders of Ayr in the same province.

Nova Scotia Canada. The Canadian province was first known as Acadia when it was settled by the French in 1604, which is probably a name of Indian origin. The territory was then granted by James I in 1621 to Sir William Alexander, Earl of Stirling (1567-1640), a Scottish poet who was a tutor to the royal family (including future Charles I). The conveyance included words referring to "the lands between New England and Newfoundland to be Known as Nova Scotia, or New Scotland", and it was the Latin version of the name that prevailed. It did not appear on the map until 1713, when after years of dispute and wrangling between the French and the English, the French finally built the powerful fortress of Louisourg on the eastern coast of Cape Breton Island and the ownership was finally settled; the French retained this island and certain other areas, while most of the territory was ceded to the English. Or rather the Scots, for many Scottish names can still be found in the province today, such as New Glasgow, Inverness, and Waverley.

Oban Scotland Argyll. Lat56.25N Long5.28W *pop.* 8,203 (1991) The main port to the Hebrides.

Oban Canada Saskatchewan.

Oban New Zealand Stewart

Island. *pop.* c.230 (1945) Capital of Stewart Island. Until the 1940s called Half Moon Bay. It is possible that Sir William Stewart, who gave his name to the Island, came from Oban.

Oban Nigeria. Town in Calabar province, Eastern Provinces, SE Nigeria. Agricultural trade centre; hardwood, rubber, palm oil and kernels, cocoa, kola nuts. Oban Hills are nearby.

Oban South Africa Transvaal. May be named by the Patterson brothers who surveyed a railway line between Springs and Bethal. They are rumoured to have emigrated from Scotland.

Oban Hills Nigeria. 30 miles long (N–S) rise to c.3500 ft. Calabar River rises on western slopes.

Orbost Scotland Isle of Skye. Lat57.24N Long6.34W 4 miles south east of Dunvegan.

Orbost Australia Victoria. The town was proclaimed in 1885. Named after a small village on the Scottish Isle of Skye, with which a settler had links.

Orcadia Scotland Isle of Bute. Lat55.50N Long5.02W

Orcadia Canada Saskatchewan. According to some books Orcadia in Saskatchewan was named from the classical name of the Orkney Islands. The area was chosen

by Scottish emigrants from the Islands, and they prefered the Latin name to the English. Perhaps they were influenced by the similar name of Nova Scotia. However Orcadia is a settlement on the Isle of Bute east of Rothesay and it is possible emigrants could have come from here.

Orkney Scotland. A group of 67 islands, one third of which are inhabited, which boast the largest concentration of prehistoric monuments in northern Europe. The first colonists arrived around 3500BC and built homes on Papa Westray which are the oldest surviving dwellings recorded in Britain. There are two henge monuments in Orkney, one at Stenness which contained twelve standing stones and the other the Ring of Brogar consisted of sixty stones. The capital of Orkney, Kirkwall became a royal burgh in 1486.

Orkney Springs USA Virginia. Situated in Shenandoah County. Health resort with mineral springs near Marrisonburg in foothills of the Alleghenies.

Orkney Springs South Africa Transvaal. Orkney is a goldmining town on the Vaal River. It was directly named after a coal mine which was on a farm owned by a Scotsman named Jackson, who came from the Orkney Islands. The town was proclaimed in 1940, although Jackson's farm had been here some time earlier in the 1880s. On 12th May 1995 a major disaster at the Vaal Reefs goldmine in Orkney killed up to 100 miners.

Orkney Canada Saskatchewan.

Paisley Scotland Renfrewshire. Lat55.50N Long4.25W *pop.* 75,526 (1991) Seven miles west of Glasgow. Largest town in Great Britain, which in the nineteenth century had a larger population than Aberdeen and Dundee. Became famous for the Paisley Pattern, the design motif on the town's silks and cotton.

Paisley Canada Ontario. Lat44.1N Long81.16W *pop.* c.900 (1994) Village situated on Saugeen River at confluence of North and South Rivers. 25 miles SW of Owen Sound.

Paisley USA Florida. Lat28.58 N Long81.32 W Small community near Lanark Village in Florida which was founded in the late eighteenth century as a beach front for the Lanark-on-the-Gulf resort.

Paisley USA Oregon. Lat42.40N Long120.34W *pop.* 214 (1950) Town in Lake County 35 miles NNW of Lakeview at altitude of 4,369 ft. Ranching area.

Paisley Pond USA Oklahoma.

Patna Scotland Ayrshire. Lat55.22N Long4.30W *pop.* 2,387 (1991) Former coal mining village.

Perth Scotland Perthshire. Lat56.24N Long3.25W *pop.* 41,453 (1991) Perth has been a royal burgh since at least the thirteenth century. It is sometimes referred to as 'The Fair City' and the 'Ancient Capital of Scotland' which refers to the city's close proximity to Scone. The name is likely to have derived from the city's location at the mouth of the Tay from the words 'Aber-Tha' which became 'Bertha' in Roman times. Perth's city status is questionable as it was never a cathedral city in its own right.

Perth Australia Tasmania. Lat41.32 S Long147.09 E *pop.* 558 (1947) Town in agriculture and dairying centre 10 miles S of Launceston.

Perth Australia Western Australia. Lat31.58S Long115.49W *pop.* over 1,000,000 (1990) Capital of Western Australia. Its port Freemantle is 9 miles SW. Founded in 1829. Seaside resorts in western suburbs.

Perth Canada Ontario. Lat44.54N Long76.15W *pop.* 4,458 (1950) County seat of Lanark County. Lies on Tay River45 miles SW of Ottawa.

Industries include wool products, woodworking, manufacturing of shoes, felt, chemicals, soap, hardware.

Perth Guiana Lat63.5N Long57.49W

Perth USA Indiana. Lat39.36N Long87.09W

Perth USA Kansas. Lat37.11N Long97.33W

Perth USA New Brunswick. *pop.* c.700 (1950) Village which lies on St John River, 22 miles south of Grand Falls in lumbering, woodworking and canoe manufacturing area.

Perth USA New York. Lat42.58N Long74.12W

Perth USA North Dakota. Lat48.44N Long99.28W *pop.* 124 (1950) Village in Towner Country which lies 22 miles NW of Cando.

Perth Amboy USA New Jersey. Lat40.32N Long74.17W *pop.* 41,967 (1990) City in Middlesex County. Was the county seat of east Jersey (1686-1702) then alternate county seat of New Jersey. Settled 1683, incorporated 1718. Good harbour at mouth of Raritan River, bridged on Raritan Bay. Industries include copper smelting, oil refining, manufacturing, shipyards, dry docks, clay deposits, port of entry.

Perth County Canada Ontario. *pop.* 49,694 (1950) In southern Ontario on Thames River. County seat is Stratford.

Perthshire USA Mississippi. Lat33.58N Long90.58W *pop.* c50,000 (1950)

Perthville Australia. Lat33.29S Long149.32E

Perth Water (Swan River) Australia Western Australia. Situated in south west state. Rises as Avon River in hills near Corrigan. Flows 240 miles. Widens to Perth Water at E Perth and into Swan estuary.

Perth Water Bay Australia Western Australia.

Renfrew Scotland Renfrewshire. Lat55.52N Long4.25W *pop.* 20,764 (1991) Three miles north east of Paisley and five miles west of Glasgow. It was created a burgh in 1124 by David I and later created a royal burgh in 1396. Battle of Renfrew was fought in 1164

Renfrew Canada Ontario. *pop.* 8,134 (1990) Founded by Scots from Renfrew in the 1840s in a timbering district.

Reston Scotland Berwickshire. Lat55.51N Long2.11W Village on Eye Water.

Reston Canada Manitoba. *pop.* c.650 (1994) The Manitoba community is named after the Scottish village of Reston from which early settlers had emigrated. It is a small unincorporated community.

Riccarton Scotland Ayrshire. Lat55.36N Long4.30W Now a residential suburb of Kilmarnock.

Riccarton New Zealand South Island. A suburb of Christchurch, the name was given by two of the original settlers here, the Scottish brothers John and William Dean, and they named it after their native village of Riccarton, Ayrshire.

Rome Scotland Ayrshire. Group of houses south east of Kilmarnock.

Rothesay Scotland Isle of Bute. Lat55.50N Long5.03W *pop.* 5,264 (1991) Largest town and capital of the Isle of Bute which became a popular holiday resort in the nineteenth century. It became a royal burgh in 1401 which gives its name to the oldest Dukedom of Scotland created in 1398 for David, son of Robert III and which is currently held by the Prince of Wales. Its has one of the best examples of a medieval castle in Scotland dating from the twelfth century. The castle was captured by the Vikings in 1230 and later occupied by King Haakon of Norway.

Rothesay Canada New Brunswick. Named from one of the titles (Duke of Cornwall & Rothesay) of Edward, Prince of Wales, the future Edward VII who embarked from here for Fredricton during his royal visit of 1860.

Roxboro USA North Carolina. *pop.* 7,732 (1990) The city in North Carolina is named after the Scottish county of Roxburgh. The town was aptly named as it similarly lies at the border with Virginia. The name was suggested by a Scotsman called James Williamson.

Roxburgh Scotland Roxburghshire. Lat55.34N Long2.29W Town was a royal burgh and popular royal residence from the twelfth century when Alexander II married Marie de Courcy in 1239 in Roxburgh Castle. At this time the town was regarded as the fourth in Scotland in terms of size and importance. The castle and town were captured by the English during the fourteenth century, recaptured then taken by the English once again. The town was eventually destroyed by the Scots. Nothing remains of town or castle today. The village of Roxburgh two miles south of the castle site was not thought important and survived.

Roxburgh New Zealand South Island. *pop.* c.400 (1990) The community in south east South Island is named from its Scottish emigrant links with the county of the same name. Roxburgh became a borough in 1877.

Roxburgh County Australia New South Wales.

Rutherglen Scotland Lanarkshire Rutherglen claims to be the oldest royal burgh in Scotland having received a charter from David I. Was the main rival to Glasgow for most of its history. It was at Rutherglen that William Wallace signed a treaty with the English in 1297, and its castle, of which nothing remains, was recaptured from the English in 1305 by Robert I. From the 1975 local government reform Rutherglen became a residential district in the City of Glasgow. Now in the district of South Lanarkshire.

Rutherglen Australia Tasmania.

Rutherglen Australia Victoria. The town in Victoria, near the border with New South Wales, was named by John Wallace who emigrated from Scotland to Australia where he opened a chain of hotels in the Australian gold rush.

Rutherglen Canada Ontario.

Rutherglen New Zealand.

Rutherglen USA Virginia.

Saint Andrew Aukland England County Durham. Also known as South Church. It is a town and parish just south east of Bishop Aukland.

Saint Andrew Bay USA Florida. Irregular arm of the Gulf of Mexico in Bay County north western Florida.

Saint Andrew Channel Canada. Nova Scotia. Arm of Great Bras d'Or in Cape Breton Island. Opening on the Atlantic.

Saint Andrew County Trinidad. County in east of Trinidad.

Saint Andrews Scotland Fife. Lat56.20N Long2.47W *pop.* 11,136 (1991) The name has been traced back to the arrival of St Andrew's relics at a Pictish settlement named Kinrymont. The town is home to Scotland's first university which is normally dated back to 1412 and Bishop Henry Wardlaw's charter. St Andrews is also home to the world famous Royal and Ancient Golf Club.

Saint Andrews Canada New Brunswick. Also known as St Andrews by the Sea. *pop.* 1,652 (1991) Town and county seat of Charlotte County on headland in Passamaquoddy Bay. Fishing and golfing resort. Formerly important shipping port dealing with Great Britain and West Indies. Founded in 1783 by loyalist settlers from Maine.

Saint Andrews Canada Quebec. Village on North River near its mouth on Ottawa River.

Saint Andrews England Channel Islands. Village on Guernsey.

Saint Andrews Jamaica. Parish lies lies in Surrey County, east Jamaica. Seat is called Half

Way Tree. Lies just north of Kingston and includes western section of Blue Mountains.

Saint Andrews USA South Carolina. *pop.* 25,692 (1990) Large unincorporated district which is largely a residential suburb of Columbia.

Saint Andrews Island Gambia.

Saint Andrews Island Spain. Island in Carribean Sea off Mosquito Coast of Nicaragua, belonging to Columbia.

Saint Andrews Major Wales. Glamorgan. Village and parish.

St Kilda Scotland. 45 miles NW of North Uist which has been uninhabited since the last 35 residents relocated to the mainland in 1930. Living on a diet of seabirds, they eventually decided they could not sustain such a small community on the island.

St Kilda New Zealand. Situated in South Island within the City of Dunedin boundary and named after the small Scottish island.

Sandness Scotland Shetland Islands Lat60.18N Long1.40W Settlement 8 miles north west of Walls.

Sandnes Norway. This is a case of inward migration giving the place a name from the colonists' home. In this case Viking invaders from the tenth to the twelfth centuries naming many places around the coasts of Scotland.

Saltcoats Scotland Ayrshire Lat55.38N Long4.47W *pop.* 11,865 (1991) Town on the Ayrshire coast between Ardrossan and Stevenston Saltcoats began as a medieval salt producing and fish curing village, hence its name. Nearby coal deposits were used to boil the sea water to extract the salt. Coal was later mined and exported to Ireland but this ceased in the mid nineteenth century. Shipbuilding and handloom weaving was also carried out. After World War II the town relied on tourism and became a popular holiday resort for Glasgow's working class families.

Saltcoats Canada Saskatchewan. The community was originally named Stirling. The change was proposed by Sir Hugh Allen (1810-1882), the Scottish financier and shipowner who was one of the projectors of the Canadian Pacific Railway.

Saltcoats USA Manitoba. Crofters from the Scottish Highlands were encouraged to settle here in the 1880s.

Scone Scotland Perthshire. Lat56.25N Long3.26W *pop.* 4,533 (1991) As the town near Perth where Scottish monarchs were enthroned, it was often called the 'Ancient Capital of Scotland'. Kenneth MacAlpin made Scone his capital when he brought the Stone of Scone in c.850 AD. The block of sandstone is believed to have been brought from the Middle East in the ninth century where it was said to have been a pillow used by Jacob in Biblical times. The stone was removed from Scone by Edward I of England in 1296 and taken to Westminster. In 1950 it was removed by Scots nationalists but returned.

Scone Australia New South Wales. The town was originally known by the Scottish name of Invermein when first gazetted in 1837 but it was renamed by two old soldiers who thought it important to have a place prepared so that in the event of a major disaster the coronation stone could be housed here.

Scotch Plains USA New Jersey. *pop.* 21,160 (1991) Situated in Union County. The residential township in New Jersey was settled in 1684 by a group of Scottish emigrants and was named as much for them as for their leader, George Scott who died on the crossing from Scotland. The plains are those south of Watchung Mountains.

Scotland USA Pennsylvania.

Community in Pennsylvania, where the Scottish namer was an Alexander Thompson.

Scotland County USA Missouri. County named by a settler from Scotland.

Scotland County USA North Carolina.

Scotsburn Canada Nova Scotia. The community in Nova Scotia was originally named Rodgers Hill. It was renamed in 1867 by a Scot, Hugh Ross after his native village of Scotsburn in Ross-shire.

Shetland Islands Scotland. A group of more than 100 islands only nineteen of which are inhabited, the largest of which is Lerwick. There is evidence of settlement on the islands dating from Stone Age, Bronze Age and early Iron Age. Much in evidence are structures known as Brochs dating from Christian times. The islands were under Scandinavian rule between 875 and 1468. Industry on the islands has been diverse including herring fishing. In the early nineteenth century the manufacturing of kelp from seaweed was carried out by the islanders. Shetland ponies were bred on the islands for work in the coal mines. Main activity now is North Sea oil related work, some fishing and tourism.

Shetland Canada Ontario. Situated in Lanark County.

South Berwick USA Maine *pop.* 5,877 (1990) Situated in York County. Possibly named after North Berwick or Berwick.

South Orkney Islands Antarctica. The islands lie south of the Scotia Sea to the north east of the Antarctic Peninsula. They were discovered by British and American sealers in 1821. They were named for their proximity to the South Shetland Islands, which had been discovered two years previously.

South Shetland Islands Antarctica. The Islands lie to the north of the Antarctic Peninsula where they were discovered and named in 1819 by the British sealer William Smith, who likened their appearance and proximity to that of the Shetland Islands off the Scottish mainland.

Sterling, Mount USA Kentucky. The city of this name in Kentucky was settled in about 1790 and originally known as Little Mountain Town, from the Indian burial mound on the site. In 1792 its name was changed to Mount Stirling after the Scottish town, with the spelling later modified.

Stirling Scotland Stirlingshire. Lat56.03N Long2.36W *pop.* 30,515 (1991) Despite its position in the centre of the country and the fact that it was often the centre of government the town never became the capital. Stirling has been closely associated with both WilliamWallace who defeated an army of English at Stirling Bridge in1297 and Robert the Bruce who defeated the English at Bannockburn seventeen years later. Although it is known to have been occupied by the Romans, the first written record of Stirling dates to the twelfth century when Alexander I died in the castle. This castle was destroyed following Edward II's defeat at Bannockburn and the earliest surviving sections of the present castle date back to the 15-17th centuries.

Stirling Australia. Lat37.26S Long147.45W

Stirling Australia Northern Territory. Lat21.44S Long133.44E

Stirling Canada Alberta. Lat49.34N Long112.30W The village on Stirling Lake in south Alberta had a population of 446 in 1950. It is a railroad junction. Not named after the Scottish town but after J A Stirling, managing director of The Trusts, Executors and Securities Corporation of London, shareholders in the

Alberta Coal & Railway Co.

Stirling Canada Ontario.
Lat44.18N Long77.33W *pop.*
990 (1950) Village in south
east of Ontario. Dairying,
flour milling and woodwork
are the main industries.

Stirling Canada Quebec.
Lat47.34N Long72.54W

Stirling New Zealand.

Stirling USA New Jersey.
Lat4041N Long74.30E *pop.*
1,076 (1950) Village in Morris
County. Industries here
include manufacturing of
pencils, metal products,
clothing andclay products.
Not named after the Scottish
town but after William
Alexander (Lord Stirling) who
succeeded his father as
surveyor general.

Stirling City USA California.
Lat39.55N Long121.31W *pop.*
c.450 (1950) Butte County
north central California. It lies
in the foothills of the Sierra
Nevada. The main industry
was a match factory which
has now closed. This town
was named after a boiler at
the sawmill factory which
had the name 'Stirling
Consolidated' on it.

Stirling Creek Australia Northern
Territory.

Stirling Island Australia Solomon
Islands. Lat4.31-11.38S
Long154.11-160.14E *pop.* of
Solomon islands in 1947 was
around 160,000. Discovered
in 1567 by Mendana,

proclaimed 1893 over some
of the Solomons. 900 mile
chain of volcanic islands,
1,500 miles north of Sydney.

Stirling Range Australia Western
Australia. Extends 40 miles
parallel with south west coast
and rises to 3,640 ft, (Bluff
Knoll). Forested slopes.
National Park near Albany
with steep cliffs and wild
flowers covering 1,156 sq km.

Stirling West, Australia. Lat35.00S
Long138.4 E

Stornoway Scotland Isle of
Lewis. *pop.* 5,975 (1991)
Stornoway on the Isle of
Lewis is the Hebridean
capital. It is the only town on
the island. Its castle, the
stronghold of the MacLeods
of Lewis was detroyed in
1654 by Cromwell and his
troops.

Stornoway Canada Quebec.
Village in south of Quebec, 18
miles north west of Megantic.
Industries are dairying,
lumbering and pig raising.

Stranraer Scotland
Wigtownshire. Lat54.54N
Long5.02W *pop.* 11,348
(1991) The town at the head
of Loch Ryan became a
Burgh of Barony in 1596 and
Royal Burgh in 1617. North
West Castle which now
operates as a hotel was the
home of famous Scottish
explorer John Ross. Two piers
were built in 1820 and 1836-
40 which captured the Irish

ferry trade and Stranraer is still a major ferry port.

Stranraer Canada Saskatchewan.

Tay, River Scotland. The River Tay is the longest river in Scotland from its source to the sea. The first Tay Railway Bridge which was opened in 1878 and designed by Thomas Bouch who was knighted for his work. It collapsed on 28th December 1879 as a passenger train crossed during a storm. 75 passengers and crew died and in a subsequent inquiry it was revealed that Bouch had not allowed for wind pressure and his contractor had used improper metal castings. The stumps of his bridge can still be seen in the Tay.

Tay River Canada Ontario. River runs through town called Perth, named after the Scottish community.

Tenterfield Scotland Stirlingshire.

Tenterfield Australia New South Wales. Established 1848. The town in north east New South Wales was founded in 1848 and named after the Scottish home of one of the early settlers.

Thurso Scotland Caithness. Lat58.35N Long3.31W *pop.* 8,488 (1991) A Viking stronghold near the village was stormed by William the Lion in the twelfth century. In 1633 Thurso became a Burgh

of Barony. Main economic activity now centres on the Dounreay nuclear plant.

Thurso Canada Quebec. *pop.* 1,295 (1950) Village in south west Quebec which lies on Ottawa River 24 miles ENE of Ottawa. Lumbering, dairying and stock raising are among the industries.

Tobermory Scotland Isle of Mull. Lat56.37N Long6.04W *pop.* 825 (1991) Chief town on the Isle of Mull which is also one of Scotland's smallest burghs. The name derives from the Gaelic Tobar Mhoire which means 'Mary's Well'. Tobermory's natural harbour is one of the safest in the Hebrides. The town was built in the 1787 by the British Fisheries Society but since the decline of the herring fishing industry in the nineteenthcentury has relied on tourism. The shipwrecked Spanish Armada galleon, the *Florida* sank in Tobermory Bay in 1588 supposedly carrying £300,000 in gold bullion. It attracts treasure hunters and divers although little has been recovered as it lies buried under30ft of silt.

Tobermory Australia Queensland.

Tobermory Canada Ontario. A popular tourist resort and mecca for divers who explore the sunken ships in the town's natural harbour. Lies at the tip of Bruce Peninsula on the coast of Fathom Five National Park.

Ugie Scotland.

Ugie South Africa Cape Province. Established 1874. The town owes its origin to the Scottish missionary William Murray, who named it in 1863, after the River Ugie, Aberdeenshire. Town of Ugie grew up from the mission station.

Ugie, River Scotland Aberdeenshire. Rises 2 miles south west of New Aberdour and flows 21 miles south east to the North Sea.